finger food

The Confident Cooking Promise of Success

Welcome to the world of Confident Cooking,
where recipes are double-tested by a team
of home economists to achieve a high
standard of success—and delicious
results every time.

bay books

TEST KITCHEN PERFECTION

You'll never make a wrong move with a step-by-step cookbook. Our team of home economists has tested and refined the recipes so that you can create fabulous food in your own kitchen. Follow our easy instructions and step-by-step photographs and you'll feel like there is a master chef in the kitchen guiding you every step of the way.

All recipes are double-tested by our team of home economists. When we test our recipes, we rate them for ease of preparation. The following cookery ratings are on the recipes in this book, making them easy to use and understand.

A single Cooking with Confidence symbol indicates a recipe that is simple and generally quick to make—perfect for beginners.

Two symbols indicate the need for just a little more care and a little more time.

Three symbols indicate special dishes that need more investment in time, care and patience—but the results are worth it.

IMPORTANT

Those who might be at risk from the effects of salmonella food poisoning (the elderly, pregnant women, young children and those suffering from immune deficiency diseases) should consult their GP with any concerns about eating raw eggs.

The Publisher thanks: AEG Kitchen Appliances, Liebherr Refrigeration and Wine Cellars; Bertolli Olive Oil; Breville Holdings Pty Ltd; Chief Australia; Kitchen Aid, Sheldon & Hammond.

Front cover: Asian-flavoured crab tartlets, page 33.
Inside front cover: Prawn, noodle & nori parcels, page 88.
Back cover: Buckwheat blinis with smoked salmon, page 16.

CONTENTS

Top: Grilled prawns with tequila mayonnaise, page 92.
Bottom: Vegetable shapes with crème fraîche and fried leek, page 27.

PLAN TO PARTY

If you're having a party, you want to have just as much fun as the guests.
Easy! Simply plan ahead so that you can relax on the day.

All the finger food in this book was chosen for its suitability as party food. That's not to say that you can't serve it as an entrée or for other occasions (see the Menu ideas on pages 108–109 for suggestions); it just means that the food is easy to eat while standing. Most of the food is small enough that your guests don't have to struggle with their food, plate, glass and serviette, with dignity the loser!

WHAT'S THE OCCASION?
If you are planning a party, your first decision should be what kind of party you want to have. Will it be casual, formal, simple or lavish? Will there be a sit-down dinner to follow or will it just be drinks and canapés? Will it last for a couple of hours or all night long?

WHEN AND WHERE?
Next, you will need to work out when and where to hold your party. Obviously, the time of year will have a big impact on the venue (for example, whether it is indoors or outdoors), but it will also affect the menu. People's eating habits change with the season: we tend to eat more filling food in the colder months and prefer lighter food when the temperature rises. So let the season be your guide when planning your menu.

The time of day will also influence your catering demands. You need to consider when your guests will have last eaten a full meal and whether they will be dining after the party. Guests who have come straight from work will generally have a hearty appetite, while those who are planning to eat after the party will eat less.

YOUR GUESTS
Another factor to consider when planning your menu is your guests. It is not only the number of people you invite that is important, but also the type of people you are inviting. What food will they enjoy? A party of footballers fresh from a grand final match, for example, will probably not be satisfied by a few delicate bites. Use your discretion here; however, a good rule of thumb with a mixed crowd is to serve a couple of conservative canapés such as tarts and party pies, plus something bread-based (especially if you are serving alcohol), then follow these with a selection of more innovative canapés. It's a good idea to include at least one vegetarian option for a mixed group.

HOW MUCH TO SERVE?
One of the most important elements of party planning is making sure there is enough food. Use the following rough guide as a starting point, then think about the other factors already mentioned to make your final selection. All our recipes have serving sizes, so refer to them when planning.

For pre-dinner nibbles, serve about 3–5 pieces of food per person. For a two or three hour cocktail party, allow about 3–5 pieces per hour for each person. For a full-length party, which generally lasts about four hours, a total of 12–15 pieces of finger food per person is a generous amount. You would normally taper off the food towards the end of the party. If your party lasts for longer than four hours, serve a light supper or meal at the end.

Nibbles such as nuts and chips are not included in this calculation, but they are useful fillers at casual gatherings.

Be aware that the more formal the gathering, the less people tend to eat. Friends will tuck in at a casual party, but are more restrained at a formal event.

It's a good idea to let your friends know what kind of occasion you are planning so that they don't come expecting an evening meal and leave ravenous after a few canapés. If you are planning a two hour cocktail party, put start and finish times on the invitation; that way people will be expecting nibbles and not a full meal. If it is an all-evening affair, let them know you'll be providing food equivalent to an evening meal.

THE CANAPÉS

Whatever the size or type of your party, don't forget to consider the limitations of your equipment, time and budget. A few platters of well-chosen ideas will create more impact and give you more freedom than attempting 20 different recipes. You can always add some ready-made snacks to round out your menu.

As a general rule, if you are having between 10 and 20 guests, provide about six different canapés and for any more guests than that, offer 8–10 different types. When you pick them, try not to repeat main ingredients; for example, don't serve prawn dumplings as well as lemon grass prawns. When serving, start with a selection of cold canapés, then move onto the hot ones.

If guests are staying for the whole evening, you might want to provide one or two sweet canapés towards the end of the party to indicate that the party is ending.

BEING PREPARED

As well as trying to choose a balanced menu, be kind to yourself by picking some foods that can be prepared well ahead (even frozen), some that can be made a couple of days in advance and just one or two that need to be finished on the day. At the end of most of our recipes you will find a 'Think ahead' note that lets you know what can be done beforehand. Limit those to be made on the day to simple frying, baking or garnishing and make sure you

have some help (either a friend or hospitality agency staff) doing the last-minute touches.

Write a detailed list of what you need to buy, what can be prepared in advance and when you should do it.

Make sure you have enough equipment to make, store and serve the canapés; particularly consider refrigeration, heating and frying requirements.

PRESENTATION

At a party, presentation is just as important as the food. Apart from normal platters and trays to serve food, you can use lacquered trays, steamer baskets lined with banana leaves, platters lined with vine leaves, or sushi mats and trays lined with napkins or coloured paper (change the paper when you replenish the tray). And for the presentation of the food itself, there are sprigs of herbs, Chinese spoons and shot glasses. Whatever you choose, make sure that you have plenty—borrow from friends or hire from a catering agency, if necessary. If you know that space will be tight at the party, avoid large heavy platters that are hard to circulate.

When arranging the food, don't crowd it. Arrange one, or at the most two, kinds of canapés on a tray at a time. They look best placed in neat, evenly spaced rows on the diagonal. Lastly, don't forget to provide for the practicalities: somewhere for discarded skewers, toothpicks or napkins. You'll be amazed what a difference a little planning makes to your enjoyment of the party!

EQUIPMENT LIST

Fridge/freezer space	Plates
Baking trays	Platters and trays
Toothpicks/cocktail sticks	Serving bowls (big/small)
Spoons and forks	Ashtrays
Napkins	Small tables
Coasters	Bowls for discarded
Glasses or plastic cups	toothpicks

party starters NIBBLES

There's nothing fussy about these tasty snacks—leave them on side tables with some napkins and your guests will need no invitation to help themselves.

SEASONED POPCORN
Ready in about 15 minutes

1/4 cup (60 ml) oil
2/3 cup (150 g) popping corn
40 g butter
2/3 cup (125 g) finely chopped
   Kalamata olives
1 fresh bird's eye chilli, finely
   chopped
1 clove garlic, crushed
1 tablespoon chopped fresh parsley
1 tablespoon chopped fresh oregano
1 teaspoon grated lemon rind

Heat the oil in a large saucepan, add the popping corn and cover. Cook over medium heat, shaking occasionally, until the popping stops. Transfer to a large bowl and discard any unpopped corn. Melt the butter in a large frying pan and add the remaining ingredients. Mix, then toss through the popcorn. Serve warm. Makes a large bowl.

HONEY-ROASTED PEANUTS
Ready in about 30 minutes

350 g raw shelled peanuts
1/2 cup (175 g) honey
1 1/2 teaspoons Chinese five-spice
   powder

Preheat the oven to slow 150°C (300°F/Gas 2). Combine the ingredients in a small saucepan and warm over low heat. Spread the nuts onto a large baking tray lined with baking paper and bake for 15–20 minutes, or until golden brown. Cool before serving. Makes 2 1/2 cups.

THINK AHEAD: You can store the honey-roasted peanuts in an airtight container for up to 1 week.

VEGETABLE CHIPS
Ready in under 30 minutes

500 g orange sweet potato
500 g beetroot
500 g parsnip
oil, for deep-frying

Preheat the oven to moderate 180°C (350°F/Gas 4). Run a vegetable peeler along the length of the sweet potato and beetroot to make thin ribbons. Cut the parsnip into thin slices.
   Fill a deep heavy-based saucepan one third full of oil and heat to 190°C (375°F), or until a cube of bread dropped into the oil browns in 10 seconds. Cook the vegetables in batches for about 30 seconds, or until golden and crisp, turning with tongs, if necessary. Drain on crumpled paper towels and season with salt. Keep warm on a baking tray in the oven and cook the remaining chips. Makes a large bowl.

PARMESAN WAFERS
Ready in about 30 minutes

1¼ cups (125 g) good-quality grated
   Parmesan
1 tablespoon flour
2 tablespoons fresh thyme

Preheat the oven to hot 220°C
(425°F/ Gas 7). Line two baking trays
with baking paper and, using a 7 cm
cutter as a guide, draw circles on
the paper. Turn the paper upside
down on the trays. Toss the cheese
and flour together in a bowl, then
sprinkle 2 teaspoons of the mixture
over 3–4 circles on the paper,
spreading the mixture to the edge
of each round. Scatter a few thyme
leaves over each round.
   Bake in batches for about
3 minutes, or until melted but not
firm. Using an egg-flip, turn the
rounds over and cook for a minute
more, or until they are firm and light
golden. Remove each round from the
tray and drape over a rolling pin or
bottle until cool. Repeat with the rest
of the ingredients. Makes 30.

CURRIED NUTS
Ready in about 30 minutes

500 g mixed nuts (almonds, brazil
   nuts, pecans, macadamias,
   cashew nuts)
1 egg white
2 tablespoons curry powder
1 teaspoon ground cumin

Preheat the oven to slow 150°C
(300°F/Gas 2). Spread the nuts in a
single layer on a baking tray and
roast for 10 minutes. Whisk the egg
white until frothy, then add the nuts,
curry powder, cumin and 1 teaspoon
salt. Toss together and return to the
oven for a further 10–15 minutes,
then allow to cool. Makes 4¹/2 cups.

MARINATED OLIVES
Prepare a day ahead

150 g Kalamata olives
150 g good-quality green olives
³/4 cup (185 ml) extra virgin olive oil
2 sprigs fresh rosemary
2 sprigs fresh thyme
2 small fresh red chillies, seeded
1 large piece lemon peel
¹/2 teaspoon fennel seeds
2 fresh thyme sprigs, extra

Place the olives, oil, rosemary, thyme,
chilli, lemon peel and fennel in a large
saucepan and warm over low heat.
Transfer to a bowl and marinate
overnight at room temperature.
Remove the olives from the oil with a
slotted spoon and discard the herbs,
reserving the oil. Add the extra thyme
to the bowl with the olives before
serving. Makes 2 cups.

NOTE: Serve the oil with bread.

*From left: Seasoned popcorn, Honey-roasted
peanuts, Vegetable chips, Parmesan wafers,
Curried nuts, Marinated olives.*

party starters DIPS

Dips are one of the easiest options for feeding the hordes at a party. They can be made well in advance and simply need to be placed on a side table for your guests to help themselves.

GUACAMOLE
Ready in under 15 minutes

2 large ripe avocados
2 tablespoons lime juice
1 tomato, seeded and finely diced
1 fresh red chilli, finely chopped
2 tablespoons finely diced red onion
1½ tablespoons chopped fresh
    coriander leaves
1½ tablespoons sour cream
1 tablespoon olive oil
½ teaspoon ground cumin
pinch of cayenne pepper

Put the avocado and lime juice in a large bowl, then mash. Stir in the diced tomato, chilli, onion, coriander, sour cream, olive oil and cumin. Season with cayenne pepper and some salt and pepper. Spoon into a serving bowl and sprinkle with cayenne pepper. Makes 2 cups.

Ideal with crudités, tortilla shards (see pages 12–15) or corn chips.

TARAMASALATA
Ready in under 15 minutes

4 slices white bread, crusts removed
⅓ cup (80 ml) milk
200 g smoked cod or grey mullet roe
1 egg yolk
1 clove garlic, crushed
150–170 ml olive oil
2 tablespoons lemon juice
1 tablespoon finely chopped fresh
    parsley

Soak the bread in milk for 5 minutes. Squeeze out the excess liquid and transfer to a food processor. Add the roe, egg yolk and garlic and process until smooth. With the motor running, slowly pour in the oil, stopping when the dip is thick and holds its form. Add the lemon juice and parsley. Season and add more lemon juice, if needed. Makes 1⅔ cups.

Ideal with crudités (see page 13) or plain bruschetta (see page 94).

NOTE: You can add a few drops of red food colouring to deepen the colour.

WARM CHEESE DIP
Ready in about 15 minutes

40 g butter
3 spring onions, finely chopped
2 jalapeño chillies, finely chopped
½ teaspoon ground cumin
¾ cup (185 g) sour cream
2 cups (250 g) grated Cheddar
green Tabasco, to drizzle

Melt the butter in a saucepan and add the spring onion, chilli and cumin. Cook without browning over low heat, stirring often, for 6–8 minutes. Stir in the sour cream and, when it is warm, add the Cheddar. Stir constantly until the cheese melts and the mixture is glossy and smooth. Transfer to a bowl, drizzle with a little Tabasco and serve warm. Makes 2 cups.

Ideal with Parmesan puff straws or tortilla shards (see pages 12–15).

RED CAPSICUM SKORDALIA
Ready in about 30 minutes

1 large floury potato (e.g. russet,
    King Edward), cut into large
    cubes
2 large red capsicums, seeded
    and cut into large flattish pieces
100 g slivered almonds, toasted
4 cloves garlic, crushed
200 ml olive oil
2 tablespoons red wine vinegar

Boil the potato until tender, then
drain and return to the pan. Mash
with a potato masher, then cool.

Meanwhile, put the capsicum,
skin-side-up, under a hot grill and
cook until the skin blackens and
blisters. Transfer to a plastic bag
and leave to cool. Peel the skin and
roughly chop the flesh. Finely grind
the nuts in a food processor, then add
the garlic and capsicum. Blend until
smooth. With the motor running,
slowly add the oil, then mix in the
vinegar. Transfer to a bowl and fold
in the mashed potato. Mix well.
Makes 2½ cups.

Ideal with crudités, orange sweet
potato wedges or deep-fried cheese
ravioli (see pages 12–15).

BABA GANOUJ
Ready in about 1 hour 30 minutes

2 eggplants (1 kg)
⅓ cup (80 ml) lemon juice
2 tablespoons tahini
1½ tablespoons olive oil
3 cloves garlic, crushed
½ teaspoon ground cumin
pinch of cayenne pepper
1 tablespoon finely chopped fresh
    flat-leaf parsley
black olives, to garnish

Preheat the oven to moderately hot
200°C (400°F/Gas 6). Pierce the
eggplants a few times with a fork,
then cook over an open flame
for about 5 minutes, or until the
skin is black and blistered all over.

Transfer the eggplant to a roasting
tin and bake for 35–40 minutes, or
until soft and wrinkled.

Place in a colander over a bowl to
drain off any bitter juices and stand
for 30 minutes, or until cool.

Carefully peel the skin from the
eggplant, and place the flesh in a
food processor with the lemon juice,
tahini, oil, garlic, cumin and cayenne.
Process until smooth and creamy.
Season to taste with salt and stir in

the chopped parsley. Spread onto a
serving plate and garnish with the
olives. Makes 1⅔ cups.

Ideal served with tortilla shards
(see page 14).

*From left: Guacamole, Taramasalata,
Warm cheese dip, Red capsicum skordalia,
Baba ganouj.*

HUMMUS
Prepare a day ahead

200 g dried chickpeas
1/3 cup (80 ml) olive oil
3–4 tablespoons lemon juice
2 cloves garlic, crushed
2 tablespoons tahini
1 tablespoon ground cumin

Soak the chickpeas in water for
8 hours or overnight. Drain. Place
in a saucepan, cover with cold water,
bring to the boil and boil for
50–60 minutes. Drain, reserving
3/4–1 cup (185–250 ml) of the
cooking liquid.

Place the chickpeas in a food
processor with the oil, lemon juice,
garlic, tahini, cumin and 1/2 teaspoon
salt. Blend well until the mixture
begins to look thick and creamy.
With the motor running, gradually
add the reserved cooking liquid
until the mixture reaches the desired
consistency. Makes 21/2 cups.

Ideal with herbed lavash, herb
grissini, crudités (see pages 12–15)
or pitta bread.

GREEN MEXICAN SALSA
Ready in under 15 minutes

300 g can tomatillos, drained
(see Note)
1 small onion, chopped
1 jalapeño chilli, finely chopped
3 cloves garlic, crushed
2 tablespoons chopped fresh
coriander leaves
1–2 teaspoons lime juice

Place the tomatillos in a food
processor with the onion, chilli,
garlic and 1 tablespoon of the
coriander. Process until smooth, then
blend in the lime juice to taste. Add
the rest of the coriander and process
just long enough to mix it through
the dip. Makes 2 cups.

Ideal served with tortilla shards
(see page 14) or corn chips.

NOTE: Tomatillos resemble green
tomatoes with a papery husk. They
are extensively used in Mexican
cooking.

WHITE BEAN DIP
Ready in under 15 minutes

2 x 400 g cans lima or cannellini
beans, drained and rinsed
1/2 cup (125 ml) olive oil
1/3 cup (80 ml) lemon juice
3 cloves garlic, finely chopped
1 tablespoon finely chopped fresh
rosemary

Place the beans in a food processor
with the oil, lemon juice, garlic and
rosemary and 1 teaspoon salt. Process
until smooth, then season with
cracked black pepper. Makes 3 cups.

Ideal with herb grissini, orange
sweet potato wedges, tortilla shards
(see pages 12–15), plain bruschetta
(see page 94) or Turkish bread.

THINK AHEAD: This dip improves
with age, so you can make it up to
2 days ahead of time.

DHAL
Ready in about 30 minutes

1 cup (250 g) red lentils, rinsed
¼ teaspoon ground turmeric
1 tablespoon oil
1 tablespoon cumin seeds
½ teaspoon brown mustard seeds
1 onion, finely chopped
1 tablespoon grated fresh ginger
2 long fresh green chillies, seeded
   and finely chopped
⅓ cup (80 ml) lemon juice
2 tablespoons finely chopped fresh
   coriander leaves

Place the lentils in a saucepan with
3 cups (750 ml) cold water. Bring to
the boil, then reduce the heat and stir
in the turmeric. Simmer, covered, for
20 minutes, or until tender.

   Meanwhile, heat the oil in a
saucepan over medium heat, and
cook the cumin and mustard seeds
for 5–6 minutes, or until the seeds
begin to pop. Add the onion, ginger
and chilli and cook for 5 minutes, or
until the onion is golden. Add the
lentils and ½ cup (125 ml) water.
Season with salt, reduce the heat and
simmer for 10 minutes. Spoon into
a bowl, stir in the lemon juice and
garnish with coriander. Makes 3 cups.

   Ideal with herbed lavash, spicy
poppadoms (see pages 12–15) or chips.

WARM CRAB AND
LEMON DIP
Ready in about 30 minutes

80 g butter
2 cloves garlic, crushed
3 French shallots, thinly sliced
1 teaspoon mustard powder
½ teaspoon cayenne pepper
½ cup (125 ml) cream
150 g cream cheese
½ cup (60 g) grated Cheddar
350 g can crab meat, drained
2 tablespoons lemon juice
2 teaspoons Worcestershire sauce
3 teaspoons chopped fresh tarragon
½ cup (40 g) fresh breadcrumbs
1 tablespoon chopped fresh parsley

Preheat the oven to warm 170°C
(325°F/Gas 3). Melt half the butter in
a saucepan, then cook the garlic and
shallots for 2–3 minutes, or until just
softened. Add the mustard powder,
cayenne pepper and cream. Bring to
a simmer and slowly whisk in the
cream cheese, a little at a time. When
the cream cheese is completely
incorporated, whisk in the Cheddar
and allow to cook, stirring constantly,
over very low heat for 1–2 minutes,
or until smooth. Remove from the
heat and add the crab meat, lemon
juice, Worcestershire sauce and
2 teaspoons of the tarragon. Season
to taste with salt and cracked black
pepper. Mix, then transfer to a small
baking dish. Melt the remaining
butter in a small saucepan, add the
breadcrumbs, parsley and remaining
tarragon and stir until just combined.
Sprinkle over the crab mixture and
bake for 15 minutes, or until golden.
Serve warm. Makes 2½ cups.

   Ideal with Parmesan puff straws
(see page 13), Turkish bread or Melba
toasts.

*From left: Hummus, Green Mexican salsa,
White bean dip, Dhal, Warm crab and
lemon dip.*

party starters DIPPERS

You can either serve these dippers with one of the home-made dips on the previous pages, or jazz up ready-made dips. Serve in large bowls or on platters.

DEEP-FRIED CHEESE RAVIOLI
Ready in under 15 minutes

oil, for deep-frying
300 g fresh cheese ravioli

Fill a deep heavy-based saucepan or deep-fryer one third full of oil and heat to 180°C (350°F), or until a cube of bread dropped into the oil browns in 15 seconds. Cook the ravioli in batches until golden brown. Remove from the oil and drain on crumpled paper towels. Sprinkle with salt and cracked black pepper and serve hot. Makes about 30.

Ideal with red capsicum skordalia or green Mexican salsa (see pages 8–11). Also good on their own.

MIXED ASIAN CRISPS
Ready in under 15 minutes

oil, for deep-frying
16 cassava crackers, broken into small pieces
16 round won ton wrappers
16 small uncooked plain prawn crackers (see Note)
1 sheet toasted nori, shredded

Fill a deep heavy-based saucepan or deep-fryer one third full of oil and heat to 180°C (350°F), or until a cube of bread dropped into the oil browns in 15 seconds. Deep-fry the cassava pieces until crisp. Remove with a slotted spoon and drain on paper towels. Repeat with the won ton wrappers and prawn chips. When they are all cool, combine and toss with the nori. Makes a big bowl.

Best on their own or with a Thai dipping sauce (see page 56).

NOTE: Cassava crackers are made from the flour of the dried cassava root. Available from Asian food stores.

HERBED LAVASH
Ready in about 15 minutes

½ cup (125 ml) olive oil
3 cloves garlic, crushed
6 slices lavash bread
2 teaspoons sea salt flakes
2 teaspoons dried mixed Italian herbs

Preheat the oven to moderate 180°C (350°F/Gas 4). Heat the oil and garlic in a small saucepan over low heat until the oil is warm and the garlic is fragrant but not browned. Brush the lavash bread on both sides with the garlic oil. Cut each piece of bread into eight triangular wedges and position side-by-side on baking trays. Sprinkle the upper side with the sea salt and herbs. Bake the lavash for 8–10 minutes, or until crisp. Makes about 48 pieces.

Ideal with hummus or dhal (see pages 10–11).

CRUDITES
Ready in about 15 minutes

100 g baby green beans, trimmed
170 g asparagus, trimmed and halved
100 g baby corn
24 sugar snap peas
2 heads of endive, trimmed
1 head of radicchio, trimmed
12 baby carrots, trimmed, leaving
    the leafy tops intact
2 red capsicums, sliced into 1 cm
    wide slices
fresh herbs (e.g. dill, chervil,
    coriander), to serve
lime quarters, to serve

Fill a large bowl with iced water and set it aside. Bring a large saucepan of salted water to the boil and blanch the beans, asparagus, corn and peas separately until tender, but still firm to the bite. Remove with a slotted spoon and refresh in the iced water, then pat dry. Separate the endive and radicchio leaves. Arrange all the vegetables, including the carrots and capsicum, in their groups on a serving plate with your favourite dip. Garnish with sprigs of fresh herbs and lime quarters. Makes enough for a platter.

PARMESAN PUFF STRAWS
Ready in under 30 minutes

4 sheets ready-rolled puff pastry
50 g butter, melted
1⅔ cups (165 g) finely grated
    Parmesan
1 egg, lightly beaten

Preheat the oven to moderately hot 200°C (400°F/Gas 6). Lightly brush the pastry with the butter, then sprinkle each sheet with ¼ cup (25 g) of the cheese and season with salt and pepper. Fold each sheet in half, bringing the top edge down towards you. Brush the tops of each sheet with the egg. Sprinkle each with 2 tablespoons of extra grated Parmesan and season with salt. Using a very sharp knife, cut the dough vertically into 1 cm wide strips. Transfer each of the strips to a baking tray lined with baking paper, spacing them evenly apart. Grab each end of the pastry and stretch and twist in the opposite direction. Bake in the oven for 8–10 minutes or until lightly browned. Makes 80.

Ideal with warm cheese dip or warm crab and lemon dip (see pages 8–11). Also good on their own.

From left: Deep-fried cheese ravioli, Mixed Asian crisps, Herbed lavash, Crudités, Parmesan puff straws.

TORTILLA SHARDS
Ready in under 15 minutes

2 tablespoons sweet paprika
1/4 teaspoon cayenne pepper
oil, for deep-frying
8 large flour tortillas, cut into long
    triangles

Combine the paprika and cayenne pepper in a small bowl. Fill a deep heavy-based saucepan one third full of oil and heat to 180°C (350°F), or until a cube of bread dropped into the oil browns in 15 seconds. Drop the tortilla shards in the oil in batches and deep-fry until crisp. Drain on crumpled paper towels and sprinkle lightly with the paprika mix while still hot. Serves 8–10.

Ideal with guacamole, baba ganouj, green Mexican salsa or white bean dip (see pages 8–11).

SPICY POPPADOMS
Ready in about 15 minutes

3 green cardamom seeds
1 1/2 tablespoons coriander seeds
1 tablespoon cumin seeds
2 cloves
1 teaspoon black peppercorns
1 bay leaf, crushed
1 teaspoon ground mace
1/4 teaspoon ground cinnamon
pinch of ground chilli
oil, for deep-frying
24 large poppadoms, broken into
    quarters

Toast the cardamom, coriander and cumin seeds, cloves, peppercorns and bay leaf in a dry frying pan over low heat for 2–3 minutes, or until richly fragrant. Cool for 5 minutes, then grind to a fine powder. Stir in the mace, cinnamon and chilli.

Fill a wide, large saucepan one third full with oil and heat to 180°C (350°F), or until a cube of bread dropped into the oil browns in 15 seconds. Deep-fry the pieces of poppadom, a few at a time, until crisp and golden. Drain on crumpled paper towels and sprinkle with the spice mix while still hot. Makes a large bowl.

Ideal with dhal (see page 11).

ORANGE SWEET POTATO WEDGES
Ready in about 30 minutes

1.3 kg orange sweet potato, peeled
    and sliced into 6 cm x 2 cm
    wedges
2 tablespoons olive oil
1 tablespoon fennel seeds
1 tablespoon coriander seeds
1/2 teaspoon cayenne pepper
1 teaspoon sea salt flakes

Preheat the oven to moderately hot 200°C (400°F/Gas 6). Place the sweet potato in a large baking dish and toss with the oil. In a mortar and pestle pound together the fennel and coriander seeds until they are roughly crushed. Add to the orange sweet potato along with the cayenne and sea salt flakes. Toss well and bake for about 30 minutes, or until browned and crisp. Serve warm. Serves 6–8.

Ideal with red capsicum skordalia or white bean dip (see pages 8–11). Also great on their own.

SPRING ONION FLATBREADS
Ready in under 1 hour

2 teaspoons oil
185 g spring onions, thinly sliced
1 clove garlic, crushed
½ teaspoon grated fresh ginger
1¾ cups (215 g) plain flour
1½ tablespoons chopped fresh
    coriander
oil, for shallow-frying

Heat the oil in a frying pan, and cook the spring onion, garlic and ginger for 2–3 minutes, or until soft.

Combine the flour and 1 teaspoon salt in a bowl. Stir in the onion mixture and the chopped coriander. Gradually stir in 1 cup (250 ml) boiling water, stopping when a loose dough forms. Knead the dough with floured hands for 1½–2 minutes, or until smooth. Cover with plastic wrap and rest for 30 minutes. Break off walnut-sized pieces of dough and roll out into thin ovals.

Fill a large frying pan with 2 cm oil and heat over medium heat. When shimmering, cook the breads 2–3 at a time for 25–30 seconds each side, or until crisp and golden. Drain on paper towels and serve warm. Makes 40.

Ideal with dhal (see page 11).

HERB GRISSINI
Ready in under 2 hours

7 g sachet dried yeast
1 teaspoon sugar
4 cups (500 g) plain flour
¼ cup (60 ml) olive oil
½ cup (15 g) chopped fresh
    flat-leaf parsley
¼ cup (15 g) chopped fresh basil
2 teaspoons sea salt flakes

Combine the yeast, sugar and 1¼ cups (315 ml) warm water in a small bowl and leave in a warm place for 5–10 minutes, or until foamy.

Sift the flour and 1 teaspoon salt into a bowl. Stir in the yeast and oil to form a dough, adding more water if necessary. Gather into a ball and turn out onto a lightly floured surface. Knead for 10 minutes, or until soft and elastic. Add the herbs, and knead for 1–2 minutes to incorporate evenly. Place the dough in a lightly oiled bowl and cover with plastic wrap. Leave in a warm place for 1 hour, or until doubled in volume. Preheat the oven to very hot 230°C (450°F/Gas 8) and lightly grease two large baking trays.

Punch down the dough and knead for 1 minute. Divide into 24 portions, and roll each portion into a 30 cm long stick. Place on the trays and lightly brush with water. Sprinkle with the salt flakes. Bake for 15 minutes, or until crisp and golden. Makes 24.

Ideal with white bean dip or hummus (see page 10).

From left: Tortilla shards, Spicy poppadoms, Orange sweet potato wedges, Spring onion flatbreads, Herb grissini.

15

BUCKWHEAT BLINI
WITH SMOKED SALMON

Preparation time: 25 minutes +
    45 minutes standing
Cooking time: 15 minutes
Makes about 40

7 g sachet dried yeast
pinch of sugar
1 cup (250 ml) warm milk
3/4 cup (100 g) buckwheat flour
1/2 cup (60 g) plain flour
2 eggs, separated
20 g butter
1/3 cup (80 ml) oil
150 ml crème fraîche
300 g smoked salmon, cut into
    2 cm strips
50 g salmon roe
fresh dill sprigs, to garnish

1 Place the yeast and sugar in a small bowl and gradually stir in the milk. Sift the flours into a large bowl and make a well in the centre. Add the egg yolks and warm milk mixture and whisk until combined and smooth. Cover and stand in a warm place for 45 minutes to prove.
2 Melt the butter, then stir into the proved dough and season. Place the egg whites in a clean dry bowl and beat with electric beaters until soft peaks form. Fold one third of the egg whites into the batter until just mixed. Gently fold in the remaining egg whites until just combined.
3 Heat 1 tablespoon of the oil in a large frying pan over medium heat. Drop 1/2 tablespoon of batter into the pan for each blini. Cook for

1 minute, or until bubbles form on the surface. Turn over and cook for 30 seconds, or until golden. Repeat with the remaining batter to make about 40 blini, adding more oil when needed. Cool completely.
4 Spread 1 teaspoon of crème fraîche on each blini, then arrange a strip

of smoked salmon over it. Spoon 1/4 teaspoon of salmon roe on top. Garnish with a sprig of dill and serve.

THINK AHEAD: The blini can be made a day in advance and stored in an airtight container. Assemble just before serving.

Keep the batter covered in a warm place until it has doubled in size.

Gently fold the egg whites through the batter until it is just combined.

Cook the blini until bubbles form on the surface, then turn over.

STUFFED BLACK OLIVES

Preparation time: 30 minutes +
  2 hours refrigeration
Cooking time: 10 minutes
Makes 36

36 pitted jumbo black or large
  Kalamata olives (see Note)
100 g goat's cheese
1 teaspoon capers, drained and
  finely chopped
1 clove garlic, crushed
1 tablespoon chopped fresh
  flat-leaf parsley
1½ tablespoons plain flour
2 eggs, lightly beaten
1 cup (100 g) dry breadcrumbs
1 tablespoon finely chopped fresh
  flat-leaf parsley, extra
oil, for deep-frying

1 Carefully cut the olives along the open cavity so they are opened out, but still in one piece.
2 Mash the goat's cheese, capers, garlic and parsley together in a small bowl, then season. Push an even amount of the mixture into the cavity of the olives, then press them closed.
3 Put the flour in one small bowl, the egg in another and combine the breadcrumbs and extra parsley in a third. Dip each olive first into the flour, then into the egg and, finally, into the breadcrumbs. Put the crumbed olives on a plate and refrigerate for at least 2 hours.
4 Fill a deep heavy-based saucepan or deep-fryer one third full of oil and heat to 180°C (350°F), or until a cube of bread dropped into the oil

browns in 15 seconds. Cook the olives in batches for 1–2 minutes, or until golden brown all over; you may need to turn them with tongs or a long-handled metal spoon. Drain on crumpled paper towels and season. Serve warm or at room temperature with lemon wedges.

NOTE: If you can't find large pitted olives, buy stuffed ones and remove the filling.
THINK AHEAD: The olives can be stuffed up to 2 days in advance and crumbed the day before you are serving them. They are best cooked on the same day they will be eaten.

Carefully split open the olives without cutting all the way through.

Stuff the olives with a small amount of the filling, then push the olives closed.

Generously coat the stuffed olives in the breadcrumb mixture.

CHICKEN SAN CHOY BAU

Preparation time: 25 minutes
Cooking time: 10 minutes
Makes about 36

1½ tablespoons vegetable oil
¼ teaspoon sesame oil
3 cloves garlic, crushed
3 teaspoons grated fresh ginger
6 spring onions, thinly sliced
500 g chicken mince
100 g drained water chestnuts,
    finely chopped
100 g drained bamboo shoots,
    finely chopped
¼ cup (60 ml) oyster sauce
2 teaspoons soy sauce
¼ cup (60 ml) sherry
1 teaspoon sugar
4 small witlof heads, bases trimmed
oyster sauce, to serve

1 Heat the oils in a wok or large frying pan, add the garlic, ginger and half the spring onion and stir-fry over high heat for 1 minute. Add the mince and continue cooking for 3–4 minutes, or until just cooked, breaking up any lumps.

2 Add the water chestnuts, bamboo shoots, oyster and soy sauces, sherry, sugar and the remaining spring onion. Cook for 2–3 minutes, or until the liquid thickens a little.

3 Allow the mixture to cool slightly before dividing among the witlof leaves; you will need about 2 heaped teaspoons per leaf. Drizzle with oyster sauce and serve immediately.

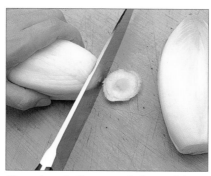

Use a sharp knife to trim the bases of the witlof heads.

THINK AHEAD: The filling can be made up to 2 days in advance and reheated just before assembling.
VARIATIONS: Pork mince is another popular choice for san choy bau: you can either swap it directly for the chicken mince or use half of each and mix them together.

There are also several types of leaves that work well for cupping the filling. Try the small leaves from a cos or iceberg lettuce or, for a more sophisticated option, try betel leaves from the betel nut tree.

Stir-fry the chicken mince, making sure you break up any lumps.

SPICED CARROT SOUP SIP

Preparation time: 30 minutes
Cooking time: 1 hour 10 minutes
Serves 36 (Makes 1.25 litres)

1/3 cup (80 ml) olive oil
2 teaspoons honey
3 teaspoons ground cumin
3 teaspoons coriander seeds, lightly
  crushed
2 cinnamon sticks, broken in half
1.5 kg carrots, cut into even chunks
  (about 3 cm)
3 cups (750 ml) chicken stock
100 ml cream
3/4 cup (185 g) sour cream
3 tablespoons fresh coriander leaves

1 Preheat the oven to moderately hot 200°C (400°F/Gas 6). Combine the oil, honey, cumin, coriander seeds, cinnamon sticks, 1 teaspoon salt and plenty of cracked black pepper in a roasting tin. Add the chunks of carrot and mix well to ensure that all the carrot is coated in the spice mixture.
2 Roast for 1 hour, or until the carrot is tender, shaking the pan occasionally during cooking. Remove from the oven, discard the cinnamon sticks with tongs and allow the carrot to cool slightly.
3 Transfer half the carrot chunks, 1½ cups (375 ml) of the stock and 1 cup (250 ml) water to a food processor or blender and blend until smooth. Strain through a fine sieve into a clean saucepan. Repeat with the remaining carrots, stock and another 1 cup (250 ml) water. Bring the soup to a simmer and cook for 10 minutes. Add the cream and season to taste. Ladle into a jug, then pour into shot glasses or espresso cups. Garnish each cup with 1/4 teaspoon sour cream and a coriander leaf.

THINK AHEAD: The soup can be refrigerated for 2 days or frozen before the cream is added for up to 8 weeks. Reheat in a saucepan. Bring to the boil, then simmer for 1 minute.

Stir the carrots into the spice mixture so that they are well coated.

Blend the carrots, stock and water until the mixture is smooth.

MINI BISTEEYA

Preparation time: 30 minutes
Cooking time: 55 minutes
Makes 24

1 tablespoon olive oil
125 g unsalted butter, melted
1 small onion, finely chopped
2 small chicken breast fillets
   (300 g in total)
2 cloves garlic, crushed
1 large cinnamon stick
¼ teaspoon ground turmeric
1 teaspoon grated fresh ginger
4–5 threads saffron
1 cup (250 ml) chicken stock
2 eggs, beaten
⅓ cup (55 g) sultanas
⅓ cup (50 g) chopped toasted
   almonds
4 tablespoons chopped fresh
   coriander leaves
9 sheets filo pastry
1 tablespoon icing sugar
2 teaspoons ground cinnamon

1 Lightly grease 24 non-stick mini muffin holes. Preheat the oven to moderate 180°C (350°F/Gas 4) and put a baking tray in the oven to warm.
2 Place the oil and 2 teaspoons of the butter in a large frying pan, add the onion and cook over medium heat for 4–5 minutes, or until just soft, then add the chicken, garlic, cinnamon stick, turmeric, ginger, saffron and stock. Bring to the boil, then reduce the heat to low and poach the chicken for 10 minutes, or until just cooked. Remove the chicken from the pan and set aside to cool.
3 Return the pan to the heat and boil until the sauce reduces to ⅓ cup (80 ml). Remove the cinnamon stick and reduce the heat to low. Add the egg to the sauce and cook, stirring constantly with a wooden spoon, for 3–4 minutes, or until the egg is set—the mixture will look curdled, but this is fine. Remove from the heat. Finely shred the chicken, then add to the pan along with the sultanas, toasted almonds and coriander. Season and allow to cool.

4 Keeping the filo covered while you work, take one sheet, brush lightly with the remaining melted butter, cover with another sheet and repeat until you have three buttered sheets. Using a sharp knife, cut 12 squares, each 8 cm. Push each of the squares down into a mini muffin hole. Fill each hole with 1 tablespoon of the chicken mixture. Repeat with another 3 sheets and the rest of the filling.
5 Layer three more sheets of filo pastry on a work surface, buttering each layer as before. Using a 5 cm cutter, cut out 24 rounds. Place these

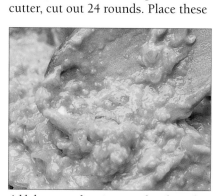

Add the egg to the mixture and cook until the egg is set.

layered rounds on top of the chicken mixture, but leave the corners of the pastry base sticking up. Use some of the melted butter to seal the top. Bake on the heated baking tray for 20–25 minutes, or until golden. Cool for 5–10 minutes before dusting with the combined icing sugar and cinnamon, then serve.

THINK AHEAD: The filling can be made up to 2 days earlier. You can assemble these the day before, but make sure they are well covered with plastic wrap or they will dry out.

Spoon the chicken filling into the muffin holes.

CUCUMBER CUPS WITH THAI BEEF SALAD

Preparation time: 30 minutes
Cooking time: 5 minutes
Makes 24

4 Lebanese cucumbers
oil, for pan-frying
250 g beef fillet steak
½ red onion, finely chopped
20 fresh mint leaves, finely chopped
1 tablespoon finely chopped fresh
    coriander leaves
1½ tablespoons fish sauce
1½ tablespoons lime juice
1 fresh bird's eye chilli, seeded and
    finely chopped
1 teaspoon grated palm sugar or
    soft brown sugar
small coriander leaves, to garnish

1 Trim each end of the cucumbers but do not peel them. Cut each cucumber into 2 cm thick slices; you should get 24 pieces. Scoop out the centre of each slice with a melon baller, leaving a shell of flesh.

2 Heat a large frying pan over high heat and brush lightly with oil. Season the beef with salt and pepper, then place in the pan and cook for 1½–2 minutes each side, depending on the thickness (the beef needs to be rare). Set aside to rest for 5 minutes. Thinly slice the beef across the grain, then slice each piece into 5 mm wide strips and transfer to a bowl.

3 Add the onion, mint and chopped coriander to the bowl and mix well. Combine the fish sauce, lime juice, chilli and sugar in a small bowl and

stir until the sugar has dissolved. Pour over the beef mixture and mix until well combined. Fill each cucumber cup with an equal portion of the Thai beef salad and garnish each one with a whole coriander leaf.

THINK AHEAD: The cups can be prepared a day early. To store them, directly cover the surface with plastic wrap to prevent them from drying out. Store in an airtight container. The meat can also be cooked a day early, but do not slice it until you are ready to assemble the salad.

Scoop out a hollow in the cucumber slices with a melon baller.

Use a sharp knife to cut the fillet steak into very thin strips.

21

RISOTTO CAKES WITH PRESERVED LEMON MAYONNAISE

Preparation time: 30 minutes +
    2 hours 30 minutes standing
Cooking time: 40 minutes
Makes 30

1 litre chicken stock
1 tablespoon olive oil
1 clove garlic, finely chopped
1 small onion, finely chopped
1 cup (220 g) arborio rice
½ cup (125 ml) dry white wine
4 marinated artichokes, drained and
    finely chopped
¼ cup (25 g) coarsely grated
    Parmesan
1 teaspoon grated lemon rind
½ cup (60 g) plain flour
2 eggs, beaten
1 cup (100 g) dry breadcrumbs
3 slices (50 g) pancetta
oil, for pan-frying
15 pitted Kalamata olives, halved
flat-leaf parsley, to garnish

Preserved lemon mayonnaise
⅓ cup (80 g) whole-egg mayonnaise
2 teaspoons finely chopped preserved
    lemon

1 Pour the stock into a saucepan and bring to the boil. Reduce the heat, cover with a lid and keep at a low simmer.
2 Heat the oil in a large saucepan and cook the garlic and onion over low heat for 4–5 minutes, or until the onion has softened. Stir in the rice for about 1 minute, or until it is well coated in the oil. Add the wine and stir over medium heat until it has all been absorbed. Add ½ cup (125 ml) of the hot stock, and stir constantly until nearly all the stock has been absorbed. Add more stock, ½ cup (125 ml) at a time, stirring constantly until it is completely absorbed before the next addition. The risotto will be ready after 20 minutes when the rice is tender and the mixture appears creamy. Stir in the artichokes, Parmesan

and lemon rind.
3 Spread the risotto out on a tray and allow to cool for 2 hours.
4 Put the flour in one bowl, the egg in another and the breadcrumbs in a third. Using wet hands, roll the risotto into 30 discs 3 cm across and 1.5 cm high. Coat them with flour, dip them in egg, then coat them in the breadcrumbs. Refrigerate for at least 30 minutes.
5 Cook the pancetta in a non-stick frying pan until crisp, then tear each slice into 10 pieces.
6 To make the preserved lemon mayonnaise, mix the preserved lemon into the mayonnaise.
7 Heat the oil in a frying pan and cook the risotto cakes in batches

for 2–3 minutes each side, or until golden and crisp. Drain on crumpled paper towels. Top each risotto cake with ½ teaspoon of the mayonnaise, a piece of pancetta, half an olive and a torn parsley leaf. The risotto cakes can either be served warm or hot.

THINK AHEAD: You can make the risotto 2 days before needed, then spread out on a tray and keep covered in the fridge until needed.

Once all the liquid has been absorbed, stir in the other ingredients.

Keeping your hands wet, roll the risotto into small discs.

BITTERBALLEN
(Dutch croquettes)

Preparation time: 30 minutes +
    overnight refrigeration
Cooking time: 40 minutes
Makes about 60

1¾ cups (440 ml) beef stock
1 small carrot, very finely diced
½ celery stick, very finely diced
1 small onion, very finely diced
1 bay leaf
50 g butter
50 g plain flour
300 g beef or veal mince
3 cloves garlic, crushed
1 tablespoon finely chopped fresh
    parsley
1 tablespoon Worcestershire sauce
2 teaspoons ground nutmeg
1 teaspoon lemon rind, finely minced
dry breadcrumbs, to coat
3 eggs, beaten
oil, for deep-frying
English mustard, to serve

1 Place the beef stock, carrot, celery, onion and bay leaf in a saucepan and bring to the boil over high heat, then reduce the heat slightly and simmer for 10 minutes. Remove from the heat, strain and set aside, reserving all the solids except the bay leaf.
2 Melt the butter over medium heat in a large saucepan, then add the flour, mix well and cook for 1 minute. Gradually add the warm stock, stirring constantly until you have a very thick, smooth sauce. Reduce the heat to low.
3 Add the mince, garlic, parsley, Worcestershire sauce, nutmeg, lemon rind, reserved vegetables, 1 teaspoon salt and ½ teaspoon cracked black pepper. Cook over low heat for 15 minutes, stirring regularly to prevent sticking. Remove from the heat, cool slightly then transfer to a clean dish. Cover and refrigerate overnight or at least until the mixture is well chilled and firm.
4 Take heaped teaspoons of the mixture and shape into balls with wet hands. Roll in the breadcrumbs, then beaten egg, then again in the breadcrumbs. Refrigerate the finished balls while you work with the rest of the mixture. If your kitchen is warm you may like to work with half of the mixture at one time so that it does not become too soft. Refrigerate the balls for at least 1 hour.
5 Fill a large heavy-based saucepan or deep-fryer one third full of oil and heat to 190°C (375°F), or until a cube of bread dropped into the oil browns in 10 seconds. Deep fry the bitterballen for 3–4 minutes, or until golden brown. Drain on paper towels and serve immediately with mustard to dip into.

THINK AHEAD: You can make the balls ahead of time and keep in the fridge for up to 2 days or freeze for up to 1 month. Thaw before cooking.

Pour the stock through a strainer, reserving the solids.

Stir the sauce until it is thick and very smooth.

SPICY CORN PUFFS

Preparation time: 25 minutes
Cooking time: 15 minutes
Makes about 36

2 corn cobs
3 tablespoons chopped fresh
    coriander leaves
6 spring onions, finely chopped
1 small fresh red chilli, seeded and
    finely chopped
1 large egg
2 teaspoons ground cumin
1/2 teaspoon ground coriander
1 cup (125 g) plain flour
oil, for deep-frying
sweet chilli sauce, to serve

1 Cut down the side of the corn with a sharp knife to release the kernels. Roughly chop the kernels, then place them in a large bowl. Holding the cobs over the bowl, scrape down the sides of the cobs with a knife to release any corn juice from the cob into the bowl.

2 Add the fresh coriander, spring onion, chilli, egg, cumin, ground coriander, 1 teaspoon salt and some cracked black pepper to the bowl and stir well. Add the flour and mix well. The texture of the batter will vary depending on the juiciness of the corn. If the mixture is too dry, add 1 tablespoon water, but no more than that as the batter should be quite dry. Stand for 10 minutes.

3 Fill a large heavy-based saucepan or deep-fryer one third full of oil and heat to 180°C (350°F), or until a cube of bread dropped in the oil browns in 15 seconds. Drop slightly heaped teaspoons of the corn batter into the oil and cook for about 1 1/2 minutes, or until puffed and golden. Drain on crumpled paper towels and serve immediately with a bowl of the sweet chilli sauce to dip the puffs into.

NOTE: The corn puffs should be prepared just before serving. The consistency of the batter changes if it is left to stand for too long and the corn puffs may fall apart when they are cooked.

Cut down the sides of the corn cobs to get all the corn kernels.

Mix the flour into the rest of the batter; the batter will be quite dry.

Fry the corn puffs until they puff up and are beautifully golden.

CAPSICUM MUFFINS WITH TAPENADE AND MASCARPONE

Preparation time: 20 minutes
Cooking time: 20 minutes
Makes 24

1 red capsicum
2 cups (250 g) plain flour
3 teaspoons baking powder
¾ cup (75 g) grated Parmesan
½ cup (125 ml) milk
2 eggs, lightly beaten
¼ cup (60 ml) olive oil
1½ tablespoons olive oil, extra
⅓ cup (75 g) mascarpone
24 fresh basil leaves

Tapenade

½ cup (80 g) pitted Kalamata olives
1 clove garlic, chopped
2 anchovies (optional)
2 teaspoons drained capers
2 tablespoons olive oil
2 teaspoons lemon juice

1 Cut the capsicum into large flattish pieces. Cook, skin-side-up, under a hot grill until the skin blackens and blisters. Place in a plastic bag and allow to cool. Peel off the skin and finely chop the flesh.
2 Preheat the oven to moderate 180°C (350°F/Gas 4). Lightly grease 24 non-stick mini muffin holes. Sift the flour and baking powder into a bowl, then add the capsicum and Parmesan. Season with salt and pepper. Make a well in the centre.
3 Pour the combined milk, eggs and oil into the well. Fold gently with a

metal spoon until just combined. Do not overmix—the batter should be lumpy. Overmixing will produce tough muffins.
4 Fill each muffin hole with the mixture. Bake for 15–20 minutes, or until a skewer comes out clean. Cool slightly. Loosen each muffin with a flat-bladed knife then lift out onto a wire rack.
5 Meanwhile, to make the tapenade, place the olives, garlic, anchovies and capers in a food processor. Blend until finely chopped, then, while the motor is running, add the oil and lemon juice to form a paste. Season with pepper.

6 Heat the extra oil in a saucepan and fry the basil leaves until they are just crisp. Remove and drain on paper towels.
7 While still warm, cut the tops off the muffins and set them aside. Spread about ½ teaspoon of mascarpone on each muffin, then add the same amount of tapenade. Put a basil leaf on the top before replacing the muffin 'lids'.

THINK AHEAD: The tapenade can be made up to 1 week in advance and stored in an airtight container in the fridge. The muffins are best if they are made on the day they are served.

Grill the capsicums until the skin blackens and blisters.

Lightly fold the batter with a metal spoon until just combined.

Fry the basil in the hot oil until the leaves are nice and crisp.

SALT AND PEPPER SQUID

Preparation time: 30 minutes +
    15 minutes marinating
Cooking time: 10 minutes
Serves 12

1 kg squid hoods, halved lengthways
    (see Note)
1 cup (250 ml) lemon juice
1 cup (125 g) cornflour
1½ tablespoons salt
1 tablespoon ground white pepper
2 teaspoons caster sugar
4 egg whites, lightly beaten
oil, for deep-frying
lemon wedges, for serving

1 Open out the squid hoods, then wash and pat dry. Lay on a chopping board with the inside facing upwards. Score a fine diamond pattern on the inside, being careful not to cut all the way through. Cut the squid into pieces measuring 5 cm x 2 cm. Place in a flat non-metallic dish and pour on the lemon juice. Cover and refrigerate for 15 minutes. Drain well and pat dry.

2 Combine the cornflour, salt, white pepper and sugar in a bowl. Dip the squid into the egg white and lightly coat with the cornflour mixture, shaking off any excess.

3 Fill a deep heavy-based saucepan or deep-fryer one third full of oil and heat to 180°C (350°F), or until a cube of bread dropped into the oil turns golden brown in 15 seconds. Deep-fry the squid, in batches, for 1 minute each batch, or until the squid becomes lightly golden and curls up. Drain on crumpled paper towels. Serve with lemon wedges.

NOTE: If you are cleaning the squid yourself, reserve the tentacles, cut them into groups of two or three depending on the size; marinate and cook them with the hoods.
THINK AHEAD: Score the squid a day ahead and store it in the fridge. Marinate and cook the squid just before serving.

Cut the squid hoods in half lengthways, then open them out so they lie flat.

Score a shallow diamond pattern on the squid, but don't cut all the way through.

VEGETABLE SHAPES WITH CREME FRAICHE AND FRIED LEEK

Preparation time: 25 minutes
Cooking time: 45 minutes
Makes 35

2 x 425 g long thin orange sweet
    potatoes, peeled
5 beetroots
1/2 cup (125 ml) crème fraîche
1 clove garlic, crushed
1/4 teaspoon finely grated lime rind
oil, for deep-frying
2 leeks, cut into thin 5 cm long strips

1 Put the orange sweet potato in one large saucepan of water and put the beetroots in another. Bring them to the boil over high heat and simmer, covered, for 30–40 minutes, or until tender, adding more boiling water if it starts to evaporate. Drain separately and set aside until cool enough to touch. Remove the skins from the beetroots. Trim the ends from the beetroots and sweet potatoes and cut both into 1 cm slices. Using a biscuit cutter, cut the thin slices into shapes. Leave to drain on paper towels.
2 Place the crème fraîche, garlic and lime rind in a bowl and mix together well. Refrigerate until ready to use.
3 Fill a deep heavy-based saucepan or deep-fryer one third full of oil and heat to 190°C (375°F), or until a cube of bread dropped into the oil browns in 10 seconds. Cook the leek in four batches for 30 seconds, or until lightly golden and crisp. Drain on crumpled paper towels and season

to taste with some salt.
4 To assemble, place a teaspoon of the crème fraîche mixture on top of each vegetable shape and top with some fried leek.

THINK AHEAD: You can make the crème fraîche mixture and deep-fry the leek a day before and keep them in separate airtight containers in the refrigerator; the garlic and lime will

infuse through the crème fraîche with the added time. If the leek softens, place on a baking tray and crisp in a hot oven for 5 minutes.

The vegetable shapes can be prepared up to 2 days in advance. Store them in the refrigerator with a sheet of plastic wrap directly on the surface to prevent them from drying out. Assemble at the last minute to avoid the crème fraîche running.

Slice the leeks into very fine strips about 5 cm long.

Slice the sweet potato and beetroot into slices about 1 cm thick.

Cook the leek in batches until it is lightly golden and crisp.

ROLLED OMELETTE WITH OCEAN TROUT CAVIAR

Preparation time: 15 minutes +
   1 hour refrigeration
Cooking time: 45 minutes
Makes 24

4 eggs
1/3 cup (80 ml) thick cream
4 tablespoons finely chopped fresh
   chives
1 tablespoon olive oil
2 tablespoons butter, melted
3 slices white bread
1/4 cup (60 g) sour cream
100 g ocean trout caviar or salmon
   roe
chopped fresh chives, to garnish

1 Whisk together one of the eggs, 1 tablespoon of the cream and 1 tablespoon of the chopped chives in a bowl and season with salt and cracked black pepper. Pour into a 25 cm lightly greased non-stick frying pan and cook over medium heat on one side for 3 minutes, or until just set; the omelettes will be difficult to roll if they are cooked for too long. Turn out onto a sheet of baking paper. Repeat with the remaining eggs and cream until you have four omelettes.

2 Tightly roll one omelette into a neat roll, then take another omelette and wrap it around the first. Repeat with the remaining omelettes so that you have two rolls. Wrap them separately in plastic wrap and refrigerate for 1 hour.

3 While the omelette rolls are being refrigerated, preheat the oven to moderate 180°C (350°F/Gas 4). Put the oil and butter in a bowl and mix them together. Using a 3 cm cutter, cut 24 rounds from the bread and brush with the butter and oil mixture. Place on a baking tray and bake for 20–30 minutes, or until crisp and golden. Remove and allow them to cool.

4 Cut each of the cooled omelette rolls into 12 rounds. Spread 1/2 teaspoon of the sour cream onto

each croûton, and sit a round of omelette on top. Top each with a teaspoon of salmon roe and garnish with a sprinkling of chopped chives.

THINK AHEAD: You can make the omelettes up to 2 days ahead of time. Store the uncut omelettes in plastic wrap in the refrigerator.

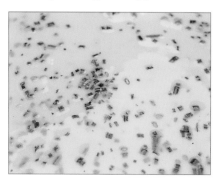

Pour the egg mixture into the pan and cook until it sets.

Tightly roll up one omelette, then roll another one around it.

HERBED FALAFEL WITH HUMMUS AND FLATBREAD

Preparation time: 40 minutes +
   overnight soaking + 30 minutes
   refrigeration
Cooking time: 35 minutes
Makes 24

100 g dried chickpeas
2 teaspoons coriander seeds
2 teaspoons cumin seeds
1¼ cups (195 g) frozen broad beans
2 tablespoons finely chopped onion
1 clove garlic, crushed
3 tablespoons chopped fresh parsley
2 tablespoons chopped fresh mint
2 tablespoons chopped fresh
   coriander leaves
oil, for deep-frying
1 piece Lebanese bread
150 g ready-made or home-made
   hummus from page 10 (use the
   rest as a dip)
4 tablespoons fresh parsley, extra

1 Soak the chickpeas in water for
8 hours or overnight. Drain.
2 Toast the coriander and cumin
seeds in a dry frying pan over low

heat for 2–3 minutes, or until
fragrant. Cool slightly then finely
grind into a powder. Add to the bowl
of chickpeas, then add the broad
beans, onion, garlic, parsley, mint,
coriander and ½ teaspoon salt to
the same bowl. Transfer to a food
processor and purée the mixture.
Using your hands, form the mixture
into flat rounds, 3–4 cm in diameter.
Place on a tray, cover and refrigerate
for 30 minutes.
3 Fill a deep heavy-based saucepan
or deep-fryer one third full of oil
and heat to 180°C (350°F), or until
a cube of bread dropped in the oil
browns in 15 seconds. Tear the
Lebanese bread into quarters and

deep-fry for 2–3 minutes, or until
crisp and golden. Remove and drain
on crumpled paper towels, then
break into small pieces.
4 Deep-fry the falafel in batches,
turning with a pair of tongs, for
3–4 minutes, or until they turn dark
golden. Remove and drain on
crumpled paper towels.
5 To serve, top each falafel round
with ½ teaspoon of the hummus,
a small piece of crisp flatbread and
a small parsley leaf.

THINK AHEAD: You can make the
falafel mixture and form the rounds,
then refrigerate, covered, for 3 days.

*Process the falafel mixture until all the
ingredients have been finely chopped.*

*Form the puréed falafel mixture into small
rounds with your hands.*

WHITEBAIT FRITTERS WITH TARTARE SAUCE

Preparation time: 20 minutes +
     1 hour refrigeration
Cooking time: 15 minutes
Makes 50

1 cup (125 g) plain flour
1 large egg, lightly beaten
1 cup (250 ml) iced water
3 tablespoons chopped fresh parsley
3 teaspoons grated lemon rind
400 g whitebait (see Note)
oil, for deep-frying

Tartare sauce
2 egg yolks
1 teaspoon Dijon mustard
1 cup (250 ml) olive oil
1 tablespoon lemon juice
2 tablespoons capers, drained and
     chopped
2 tablespoons chopped gherkins
1 tablespoon chopped fresh parsley
1 tablespoon chopped fresh tarragon

1 Sift the flour and a pinch of salt and pepper into a large bowl, make a well in the centre and add the egg. Whisk gently and gradually add the water, stirring constantly to a smooth batter. Stir in the parsley and lemon rind. Refrigerate, covered, for 1 hour.
2 To make the tartare sauce, place the egg yolks and mustard in a food processor and pulse for 10 seconds. With the motor running, slowly add the oil in a thin stream until the mixture is thick and creamy. Add the lemon juice and 2 teaspoons boiling water and pulse for another 10 seconds. Transfer to a bowl, add the capers, gherkins, parsley and tarragon and season generously. Cover and refrigerate until needed.
3 Pat the whitebait dry, then gently stir it into the batter. Fill a large heavy-based saucepan or deep-fryer one third full of oil and heat to 190°C (375°F), or until a cube of bread dropped in the oil browns in 10 seconds. Put small tablespoons of batter into the oil. Cook the fritters in batches, gently tossing in the oil.

Cook for 2–3 minutes, or until the fritters are golden brown. Drain on crumpled paper towels and keep warm. Repeat with the remaining mixture. Serve immediately with the tartare sauce.

NOTE: The most suitable 'whitebait' are very small fish, 2–3 mm wide and about 3–4 cm long, that are all white and have two small dark dots as eyes. The term whitebait can mean several varieties of fish, some of which are large and will not produce the same results. Many of these larger varieties will need trimming and cleaning.
THINK AHEAD: The tartare sauce can be made up to 3 days in advance, but stir in the fresh herbs just before you are ready to serve.

Stir the capers, gherkins, parsley and tarragon into the sauce mixture.

Add the whitebait to the batter and gently stir until completely mixed through.

cooked to your liking. Remove from the oven, cover with foil and rest for 15 minutes before slicing thinly.

5 Arrange one slice of beef on each croûte (you may need to cut the slices in half if they are too big), top with ½ teaspoon of the horseradish cream and a small sprig of fresh thyme. Serve immediately.

NOTE: Grated horseradish is readily available in small jars preserved in vinegar. Don't confuse it with horseradish sauce, which already has a cream base.

THINK AHEAD: The beef and croûtes can be prepared the day before serving. Leave the beef whole, covered, in the refrigerator and slice it just prior to assembling. Keep the croûtes in an airtight container lined with paper towels to absorb any excess oil.

VARIATION: For a spicy variation on this classic canapé, marinate the beef fillet in ⅓ cup (80 ml) olive oil, 1 teaspoon paprika, 2 cloves crushed garlic and ½ teaspoon cayenne pepper. Top with a little preserved lemon mayonnaise from page 22 or make a simple garlic cream by combining 1 clove crushed garlic with ½ cup lightly whipped thick cream and some salt and black pepper to taste.

ROAST BEEF ON CROUTES

Preparation time: 20 minutes +
    3 hours 15 minutes standing
Cooking time: 25 minutes
Makes 30

300 g piece beef eye fillet
⅓ cup (80 ml) olive oil
2 cloves garlic, crushed
2 sprigs fresh thyme plus extra to
    garnish
10 slices white bread
1 large clove garlic, peeled, extra

Horseradish cream
⅓ cup (80 ml) thick cream
1 tablespoon horseradish (see Note)
1 teaspoon lemon juice

1 Place the beef in a non-metallic bowl, pour on the combined oil, garlic and thyme and toss to coat well. Cover with plastic wrap and marinate in the refrigerator for 2–3 hours. Preheat the oven to moderately hot 200°C (400°F/Gas 6).

2 To make the croûtes, cut out three rounds from each slice of bread using a 5 cm fluted cutter. Place the rounds on a baking tray and bake for 5 minutes each side, then rub the whole garlic clove over each side of the rounds and set aside.

3 To make the horseradish cream, put the cream in a small bowl and whisk lightly until thickened. Gently fold in the horseradish and lemon juice, then season with cracked black pepper. Refrigerate until ready to use.

4 Heat a roasting tin in the oven for 5 minutes. Remove the beef from the marinade, reserving the marinade. Generously season the beef on all sides with salt and pepper, then place it in the hot roasting tin and turn it so that all sides of the meat are sealed. Drizzle with 2 tablespoons of the reserved marinade, then roast for 10–12 minutes for rare, or until

Fold the horseradish and lemon juice into the whisked cream.

Rest the beef, then thinly slice across the grain with a sharp knife.

variations on a theme TARTLETS

The beauty of these tartlets is that the pastry cases can be made ahead of time, so that you just need to make the toppings on the day. Each recipe makes 30 delicious tartlets.

BASIC PASTRY CASES

2 cups (250 g) plain flour
125 g chilled butter, chopped
1 egg

Preheat the oven to moderately hot 200°C (400°F/Gas 6). Lightly grease 30 mini muffin holes. Sift the flour into a large bowl and rub the butter in with your fingertips until the mixture resembles fine breadcrumbs. Make a well in the centre, add the egg and mix with a flat-bladed knife, using a cutting action until it comes together in beads. If the dough seems too dry, add a little cold water. Press the dough into a ball on a lightly floured surface, then wrap it in plastic wrap and refrigerate for 30 minutes.

Roll out the dough between two sheets of baking paper to 2 mm thick and cut out 30 rounds with a 6 cm cutter. Press a round into each muffin hole. Prick the bases with a fork and bake for 6–8 minutes, or until dry

and golden. If they puff up, use a clean tea towel to press out any air pockets. Cool before filling with the topping of your choice. Makes 30.

THINK AHEAD: The pastry cases can be made 2–3 days early and kept in an airtight container. If they go soft, crispen them on a baking tray in a warm (170°C/ 325°F/Gas 3) oven for 5 minutes.

CHERRY TOMATO AND BOCCONCINI
Ready in about 1 hour 30 minutes

300 g cherry tomatoes, quartered
2 tablespoons olive oil
1 clove garlic, crushed
200 g bocconcini, quartered
80 g chopped Kalamata olives
1 tablespoon extra virgin olive oil
1 tablespoon torn fresh basil
oil, for deep-frying
30 small fresh basil leaves
30 cooked tartlet cases

Preheat the oven to moderately hot 200°C (400°F/Gas 6). Combine the tomatoes, olive oil and garlic in a roasting tin and bake for 15 minutes, or until golden. Cool, then transfer to a bowl and add the bocconcini, olives, extra virgin olive oil and torn basil, then season and gently toss.

Fill a small saucepan one third full of oil and heat to 180°C (350°F), or until a cube of bread browns in 15 seconds. Deep-fry the basil in batches for 30 seconds, or until crisp. Drain. Spoon the mixture into the cases and top with a basil leaf.

CREAMED EGG WITH ROE
Ready in under 1 hour

4 eggs and 4 egg yolks
75 g unsalted butter
4 tablespoons roe
30 cooked tartlet cases

Lightly beat the eggs and egg yolks together. Melt the butter in a small

saucepan over very low heat, then add the eggs and whisk slowly and constantly for 5–6 minutes, or until the mixture is thick and creamy but the eggs are not scrambled. Remove from the heat straight away and season to taste with salt and cracked black pepper. Fill each pastry case with 1 teaspoon of the creamed egg mixture, then top with ½ teaspoon of roe before serving.

MUSHROOM RAGOUT
Ready in about 1 hour 15 minutes

50 g butter
4 spring onions, chopped
2 cloves garlic, chopped
150 g small Swiss brown or shiitake mushrooms, thinly sliced
100 g oyster mushrooms, cut into eighths
50 g enoki mushrooms, trimmed, pulled apart and sliced lengthways
3 teaspoons plain flour
2 tablespoons chicken stock or water
2 tablespoons sake
⅓ cup (80 ml) thick cream
snow pea sprouts, stalks removed
30 cooked tartlet cases

Melt the butter in a large frying pan over medium heat, add the spring onion and garlic and cook for 1 minute. Add the mushrooms and cook, stirring, for 3–4 minutes, or until soft. Add the flour and stir for another minute. Pour in the stock and sake and stir for 1 minute, or until evaporated, then add the cream and cook for 1 minute, or until thickened. Season. Spoon into the prepared pastry cases and top each one with a snow pea sprout leaf.

ASIAN-FLAVOURED CRAB
Ready in under 1 hour

¼ cup (60 ml) lime juice
1 tablespoon fish sauce
1 tablespoon grated palm sugar or soft brown sugar
300 g fresh crab meat, shredded and well drained
2 tablespoons chopped fresh coriander leaves
1 tablespoon chopped fresh Vietnamese mint
1 small fresh red chilli, finely chopped
2 kaffir lime leaves, finely shredded
30 cooked tartlet cases

Combine the lime juice, fish sauce and sugar in a bowl and stir until the sugar is dissolved. Mix in the rest of the ingredients, then spoon into the prepared pastry cases and serve.

From left: Cherry tomato and bocconcini, Creamed egg with roe, Mushroom ragout, Asian-flavoured crab.

WON TON STACKS WITH TUNA AND GINGER

Preparation time: 20 minutes
Cooking time: 10 minutes
Makes 24

1½ tablespoons sesame seeds
12 fresh won ton wrappers
½ cup (125 ml) peanut or vegetable oil
150 g piece fresh tuna fillet (see Note)
¼ cup (60 g) Japanese mayonnaise
50 g pickled ginger
50 g snow pea sprouts
2 teaspoons mirin
2 teaspoons soy sauce
¼ teaspoon sugar

1 Lightly toast the sesame seeds in a small dry frying pan over low heat for 2–3 minutes, or until golden.

2 Cut the won ton wrappers into quarters to give 48 squares in total. Heat the oil in a small saucepan over medium heat and cook the wrappers in batches for 1–2 minutes, or until they are golden and crisp. Drain on crumpled paper towels.

3 Thinly slice the tuna into 24 slices. Spoon approximately ¼ teaspoon of the mayonnaise onto 24 of the won ton squares. Place a slice of tuna on the mayonnaise and top with a little of the pickled ginger, snow pea sprouts and sesame seeds.

4 Mix the mirin, soy sauce and sugar together in a small bowl and drizzle a little over each stack. Season with pepper. Top with the remaining 24 won ton squares (lids). Serve immediately or the stacks will become soggy.

NOTE: For this recipe, you need good-quality tuna. Sashimi tuna is the best quality, but if you can't get that, get tuna with as little sinew as possible.

THINK AHEAD: The won ton wrappers can be fried the day before serving. Store them in an airtight container large enough so that they are not cramped. Place sheets of paper towels between each layer.

Cut the won ton wrappers into four equal squares.

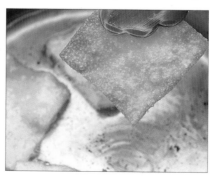

Cook the won ton squares in the hot oil until they are crisp and golden.

Using a sharp knife, cut the tuna into very thin slices.

THAI CHICKEN SAUSAGE ROLLS

Preparation time: 20 minutes
Cooking time: 15 minutes
Makes 24

200 g chicken breast fillet, roughly
    chopped
150 g mild pancetta, chopped
1 clove garlic, crushed
3 spring onions, chopped
2 tablespoons chopped fresh coriander
2 bird's eye chillies, seeded and finely
    chopped
1 teaspoon fish sauce
1 egg
1 teaspoon grated fresh ginger
375 g block frozen puff pastry
1 egg yolk
2 tablespoons sesame seeds
sweet chilli sauce, to serve
fresh coriander, to serve

1 Preheat the oven to moderate 180°C (350°F/Gas 4). Put the chicken, pancetta, garlic, spring onion, coriander, chilli, fish sauce, whole egg and ginger in a food processor and process until just combined.
2 Roll out the pastry to an oblong 30 x 40 cm. Cut in half lengthways. Take half the filling and, using floured hands, roll it into a long sausage shape and place along the long edge of one piece of pastry. Brush the edges with a little water and fold over, pressing down to seal. Place the sealed edge underneath. Repeat with the remaining pastry and filling.
3 Using a sharp knife, cut the sausage rolls into 3 cm lengths on the diagonal; discard the end pieces. Brush the tops with egg yolk, then sprinkle with sesame seeds. Bake for 10–15 minutes, or until golden. Serve with sweet chilli sauce and garnished with fresh coriander.

THINK AHEAD: You can make the sausage rolls a day before the party. Reheat in a moderate (180°C/350°F/ Gas 4) oven for 10–12 minutes, or until warmed through.

VARIATION: For spicy lamb sausage rolls, follow the method outlined for the basic sausage roll, but change the filling. Mix 375 g lamb mince, 1/2 cup (40 g) fresh breadcrumbs, 1/2 small grated onion, 2 teaspoons soy sauce, 1 teaspoon grated fresh ginger, 1 teaspoon soft brown sugar, 1/2 teaspoon ground coriander, 1/4 teaspoon each of ground cumin and sambal oelek. Lightly sprinkle the uncooked sausage rolls with poppy seeds after glazing and bake for 10–15 minutes.

Mix the filling ingredients in the food processor until combined.

Place the sausage filling along one long edge of the pastry.

SALT COD FRITTERS

Preparation time: 15 minutes +
    24 hours soaking
Cooking time: 50 minutes
Makes 28

500 g salt cod
1 large potato (200 g), unpeeled
2 tablespoons milk
¼ cup (60 ml) olive oil
1 small onion, finely chopped
2 cloves garlic, crushed
¼ cup (30 g) self-raising flour
2 eggs, separated
1 tablespoon finely chopped fresh
    flat-leaf parsley
oil, for deep-frying

1 Soak the cod in cold water for 24 hours, changing the water at least three times. Put the potato in a large saucepan of water, bring to the boil and cook for 20 minutes, or until soft. Drain. When cool enough to handle, peel the potato and mash with the milk and 2 tablespoons of the olive oil.

2 Drain the cod, cut into large pieces and place in a saucepan. Cover with cold water, bring to the boil over high heat, then reduce the heat to medium and simmer for 10 minutes, or until soft. Drain. When cool enough to handle, remove the skin and any bones, then mash with a fork until flaky. (You should have about 200 g of flesh.)

3 Heat the remaining olive oil in a frying pan, add the onion and cook over medium heat for 5 minutes, or until softened and starting to brown.

Add the garlic and cook for 1 minute. Remove from the heat.

4 Combine the potato, cod, onion mixture, flour, egg yolks and parsley in a bowl and season with cracked black pepper. Whisk the egg whites until stiff then fold into the mixture.

5 Fill a large heavy-based saucepan or deep-fryer one third full with oil and heat to 190°C (375°F), or until a cube of bread dropped in the oil

browns in 10 seconds. Drop level tablespoons of the mixture into the oil and cook for 2 minutes, or until puffed and golden. Drain on crumpled paper towels and serve.

THINK AHEAD: The cod can be prepared up to 2 days before making the fritters. Keep the flaked cod flesh in an airtight container in the fridge.

After soaking and draining, cut the cod into large pieces.

Lightly mash the cod flesh with a fork until it is flaky.

Fold the whisked egg whites into the rest of the batter.

DOLMADES

Preparation time: 40 minutes +
   25 minutes soaking
Cooking time: 45 minutes
Makes 48

200 g packet vine leaves in brine
1 cup (250 g) medium-grain rice
1 small onion, finely chopped
1 tablespoon olive oil
50 g pine nuts, toasted
2 tablespoons currants
2 tablespoons chopped fresh dill
2 tablespoons finely chopped
   fresh mint
2 tablespoons finely chopped fresh
   flat-leaf parsley
1/3 cup (80 ml) olive oil, extra
2 tablespoons lemon juice
2 cups (500 ml) chicken or vegetable
   stock

1 Put the vine leaves in a bowl, cover with cold water and soak for 15 minutes. Remove, pat dry and cut off any stems. Reserve 5–6 leaves; discard any with holes. Meanwhile, pour boiling water over the rice and soak for 10 minutes, then drain.
2 Place the rice, onion, oil, pine nuts, currants, herbs and salt and pepper in a large bowl, and mix well.
3 Lay some leaves vein-side-down on a flat surface. Place 1/2 tablespoon of filling in the middle of each leaf, fold the stalk end over the filling, then the left and right sides into the middle, and finally roll firmly towards the tip. The dolmade should resemble a small fat cigar. Repeat with the remaining filling and leaves

to make 48 dolmades.
4 Line the base of a large heavy-based saucepan or flameproof casserole dish with the reserved leaves. Drizzle with 1 tablespoon of the extra oil. Put the dolmades in the pan, tightly packing them in one layer. Pour the remaining oil and lemon juice over them.
5 Pour the stock over the dolmades and cover with an inverted plate to stop them moving while cooking. Bring to the boil, then reduce the heat and simmer gently, covered, for

45 minutes. Remove with a slotted spoon. Serve warm or cold.

THINK AHEAD: The dolmades can be prepared up to 3 days in advance and kept refrigerated in the stock after they have been cooked. If serving cold, remove them from the stock at least 1 hour before serving. If serving warm, return the dolmades to the stove in the stock and gently bring to the boil. Simmer for 2–3 minutes and remove from the stock.

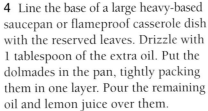

After soaking the vine leaves, pat them dry with paper towel.

Place the filling in the middle of the leaf and roll up to enclose it.

Tightly pack the dolmades into the saucepan in a single layer.

37

STUFFED CHILLIES

Preparation time: 15 minutes
Cooking time: 30 minutes
Makes 24

1 teaspoon cumin seeds
12 mild small jalapeño or similar mild
    oblong-shaped fat chillies,
    approximately 4 cm x 3 cm
1 tablespoon olive oil
2 cloves garlic, finely chopped
½ small red onion, finely chopped
½ cup (125 g) cream cheese,
    softened
¼ cup (30 g) coarsely grated Cheddar
2 tablespoons finely chopped drained
    sun-dried tomatoes
1 tablespoon chopped fresh coriander
1 teaspoon finely chopped lime rind
pinch of smoky paprika
½ cup (50 g) coarse dry breadcrumbs
2 teaspoons lime juice
coriander leaves, to garnish

1 Preheat the oven to moderately hot 200°C (400°F/Gas 6). Line a baking tray with baking paper. Toast the cumin seeds in a small dry frying pan for 1–2 minutes, or until fragrant. Cool slightly, then grind the seeds.
2 Cut the chillies lengthways through the middle. Wearing gloves, remove the seeds and membranes. Bring a saucepan of water to the boil, add the chillies and cook for 1 minute, or until the water comes back to the boil. Drain, rinse under cold water, then return to a saucepan of fresh boiling water for another minute before draining, rinsing under cold water, then draining again.

3 Heat the oil in a non-stick frying pan and cook the garlic and onion over medium–low heat for 4–5 minutes, or until the onion softens. Remove from the heat.
4 Mash the cream cheese in a bowl, add the Cheddar, sun-dried tomatoes, coriander, lime rind, paprika, cumin and half the breadcrumbs and mix well. Stir in the cooked onion and season. Fill each chilli with one heaped teaspoon of the mixture, then lay them on the baking tray and scatter

with the remaining breadcrumbs.
5 Bake for 20 minutes. Remove; squeeze some lime juice over the top and garnish with coriander leaves.

NOTE: Test the heat of the chillies by placing your tongue on the flesh after blanching twice. If they are still too hot, blanch again.
THINK AHEAD: The chillies can be stuffed the day before serving but they are best crumbed and baked on the day they are to be served.

Wearing gloves to protect your hands, remove the seeds and membrane.

Fill the chillies with a heaped teaspoon of the spicy cream cheese mixture.

Sprinkle the stuffed chillies with breadcrumbs.

MINI CORN MUFFINS WITH CAJUN FISH

Preparation time: 25 minutes
Cooking time: 25 minutes
Makes 24

Muffins
3/4 cup (90 g) self-raising flour
2 tablespoons cornflour
1/2 teaspoon baking powder
1/2 cup (75 g) fine cornmeal
2 tablespoons sugar
2/3 cup (170 ml) milk
1 egg
30 g butter, melted
20 g butter, extra

1 teaspoon onion powder
1 teaspoon dried thyme
3/4 teaspoon sea salt flakes
1/2 teaspoon garlic powder
1/4 teaspoon cayenne pepper
1/4 teaspoon dried oregano
400 g bream fillets, skinned
30 g butter
1/2 cup (125 g) sour cream
coriander leaves, to garnish

1 Preheat the oven to moderate 180°C (350°F/Gas 4). Lightly grease 24 non-stick mini muffin holes. Sift the flour, cornflour and baking powder into a bowl. Stir in the cornmeal and sugar. Make a well in the centre. Pour the combined milk and egg into the well, then the melted butter. Fold gently with a metal spoon until just combined and still a little lumpy.
2 Fill each muffin hole about three-quarters full. Bake for 15–20 minutes, or until golden. Just before removing from the oven, melt the extra butter. Brush the hot muffins generously with the melted butter, then remove from the tin and cool on a wire rack.
3 Combine the spices and herbs and 1/4 teaspoon cracked black pepper. Slice the fish into 1.5 cm slices and coat well in the spice mixture.
4 Melt the butter in a stainless steel frying pan (not non-stick) over medium heat and add the fish when the butter is foaming. Cook the fish, turning once, for 1–2 minutes, or until it starts to blacken, and is cooked.
5 To serve, cut a small wedge in the top of the muffins, then put in 1/2 teaspoon of sour cream, then add a piece of fish and a coriander leaf. Serve while the fish is hot.

THINK AHEAD: The muffins can be kept in an airtight container for 2 days or frozen for 2 weeks. Thaw, then heat on a baking tray in a warm (170°C/ 325°F/Gas 3) oven for 10 minutes.

Fold the melted butter into the bowl with the rest of the batter.

Cook the fish pieces in the hot butter until they blacken.

variations on a theme OYSTERS

Oysters whisper elegance and will set the tone for any celebration. Buy two dozen oysters, then serve with one of these delicious toppings.

BASIC OYSTER RECIPE

Buy 24 fresh oysters, remove from the shells and pat dry. Wash the shells, replace the oysters and cover with a damp cloth in the fridge. They are fabulous with a simple squeeze of lemon, or try one of these toppings.

NOTE: Oysters are sold freshly shucked on the half shell, or alive and unshucked. When buying fresh shucked oysters, look for a plump, moist oyster. The flesh should be creamy with a clear liquid (oyster liquor) surrounding it. Oysters should smell like the fresh sea and have no traces of shell particles. If you prefer to shuck them yourself, look for tightly closed, unbroken shells.

Oysters are often served on a bed of rock salt or crushed ice to help them remain stable and upright and to keep them cool in summer.

GINGER SHALLOT
Ready in about 15 minutes

2 tablespoons Japanese soy sauce
1 tablespoon mirin
2 teaspoons sake
1/2 teaspoon sugar
1 1/2 tablespoons thinly sliced fresh ginger
2 tablespoons thinly sliced spring onion
2 teaspoons sesame oil
24 prepared oysters
toasted sesame seeds, to garnish

Place the soy sauce, mirin, sake and sugar in a small saucepan and mix together well. Simmer over low heat, stirring, until the sugar dissolves, then stir in the ginger and spring onion. Simmer for a minute, then add the sesame oil. Spoon about 1/2 teaspoon of the sauce over each oyster. Garnish with sesame seeds and serve.

LEMON HERB DRESSING
Ready in about 15 minutes

1 tablespoon chopped fresh dill
1 clove garlic, crushed
1 tablespoon finely chopped fresh flat-leaf parsley
2 teaspoons finely chopped fresh chives
2 tablespoons lemon juice
1/4 cup (60 ml) extra virgin olive oil
24 prepared oysters
chive bows, to garnish
brown bread, cubed, to garnish

Place the dill, garlic, parsley, chives, lemon juice and oil in a bowl and season to taste with salt and cracked black pepper. Mix together well, then drizzle a little of the dressing over each oyster. Garnish with chive bows and serve with tiny cubes of brown bread.

TOMATO, CHILLI AND CORIANDER SALSA
Ready in under 15 minutes

2 vine-ripened tomatoes, seeded
   and finely diced
2 French shallots, finely chopped
2 small fresh red chillies, seeded
   and sliced
3 tablespoons chopped fresh
   coriander
1 tablespoon lime juice
24 prepared oysters

Place the tomato, shallots, chilli and coriander in a bowl and mix together well. Stir in the lime juice, then season with salt and pepper. Place a teaspoon of the salsa on each oyster.

PROSCIUTTO AND BALSAMIC VINEGAR
Ready in under 15 minutes

2 teaspoons olive oil
6 slices prosciutto, finely chopped
2 French shallots, finely chopped
1 tablespoon balsamic vinegar
24 prepared oysters

Heat the oil in a small frying pan over medium heat, add the prosciutto and shallots and fry until the prosciutto is crisp. Add the vinegar and cook for 1 minute to warm through. Spoon a little of the topping over each oyster.

WASABI CREME FRAICHE
Ready in under 15 minutes

1/3 cup (80 ml) crème fraîche
2 tablespoons whole-egg mayonnaise
1½ teaspoons wasabi paste
24 prepared oysters
flying fish roe, to garnish
small lime wedges, to garnish

Combine the crème fraîche, mayonnaise and wasabi paste in a bowl and whisk well. Place a teaspoon of the mixture on top of each oyster, then garnish with the roe and lime wedges.

From left: Ginger shallot, Lemon herb dressing, Tomato, chilli and coriander salsa, Prosciutto and balsamic vinegar, Wasabi crème fraîche.

LENTIL PATTIES WITH CUMIN SKORDALIA

Preparation time: 40 minutes +
    30 minutes refrigeration
Cooking time: 55 minutes
Makes 32

1 cup (185 g) brown lentils
1 teaspoon cumin seeds
1/2 cup (90 g) burghul (bulgur wheat)
1 tablespoon olive oil
3 cloves garlic, crushed
4 spring onions, thinly sliced
1 teaspoon ground coriander
3 tablespoons chopped fresh parsley
3 tablespoons chopped fresh mint
2 eggs, lightly beaten
oil, for deep-frying

Skordalia
500 g floury potatoes, cut into
    2 cm cubes (see Notes)
3 cloves garlic, crushed
1/2 teaspoon ground cumin
pinch of ground white pepper
3/4 cup (185 ml) olive oil
2 tablespoons white vinegar

1 To make the patties, place the lentils in a saucepan, add 2½ cups (625 ml) water and bring to the boil. Reduce the heat to low and cook, covered, for 30 minutes, or until soft. Meanwhile, toast the cumin seeds in a dry frying pan over low heat for 1–2 minutes, or until fragrant. Grind.
2 Remove the lentils from the heat and stir in the burghul. Set aside to cool a little.
3 Heat the olive oil in a small frying pan, add the garlic and spring onion and cook for 1 minute, then add the coriander and cumin and cook for a further 30 seconds. Stir into the lentil mixture along with the parsley, mint and eggs. Mix well. Refrigerate for 30 minutes.
4 To make the skordalia, cook the potato in a large saucepan of boiling water for 10 minutes, or until very soft. Drain the potato and mash until quite smooth. Stir in the garlic, cumin, white pepper and 1 teaspoon salt. Gradually pour in the oil,

mixing well with a wooden spoon. Add the vinegar.
5 Roll tablespoons of the lentil mixture into balls, then flatten slightly to form patties. Fill a deep heavy-based saucepan or deep-fryer one third full of oil and heat to 180°C (350°F), or until a cube of bread browns in 15 seconds. Cook the patties in batches for 1–2 minutes, or until crisp and browned. Drain on crumpled paper towels. Serve warm with the skordalia.

NOTES: Use King Edward, russet or pontiac potatoes for the skordalia.
    Do not make skordalia with a food processor—the processing will turn the potato into a gluey mess.
THINK AHEAD: Skordalia will keep in an airtight container for up to 2–3 days in the fridge. The lentil patties can be frozen uncooked for up to 2 months or refrigerated for 2 days.

Gradually pour the olive oil into the mashed potato, mixing at the same time.

Roll the mixture into balls and gently flatten with your hand to form patties.

VEGETABLE DUMPLINGS

Preparation time: 40 minutes +
    15 minutes soaking
Cooking time: 20 minutes
Makes 24

8 dried Chinese mushrooms
1 tablespoon oil
2 teaspoons finely chopped fresh ginger
2 garlic cloves, crushed
100 g Chinese chives, chopped
100 g water spinach, cut into
    1 cm lengths
¼ cup (60 ml) chicken stock
2 tablespoons oyster sauce
1 tablespoon cornflour
1 teaspoon soy sauce
1 teaspoon rice wine
¼ cup (45 g) water chestnuts, chopped
chilli sauce, to serve

Wrappers
200 g wheat starch (see Note)
1 teaspoon cornflour
oil, for kneading

1 Soak the mushrooms in 2 cups (500 ml) hot water for 15 minutes. Finely chop the mushroom caps.
2 Heat the oil in a frying pan over high heat, add the ginger, garlic and a pinch of salt and white pepper and cook for 30 seconds. Add the chives and spinach and cook for 1 minute.
3 Combine the stock, oyster sauce, cornflour, soy sauce and rice wine and add to the spinach mixture along with the water chestnuts and mushrooms. Cook for 1–2 minutes, or until the mixture thickens, them remove from the heat and cool completely.

4 To make the wrappers, combine the wheat starch and cornflour in a bowl. Make a well in the centre and add ¾ cup (185 ml) boiling water, a little at a time, while bringing the mixture together with your hands. When it is combined, immediately knead it, using lightly oiled hands until the dough forms a shiny ball.
5 Keeping the dough covered with a cloth while you work, pick walnut-sized pieces from the dough, and using well-oiled hands, squash them between the palms of your hands then roll out as thinly as possible into

circles no larger than 10 cm diameter. Place 1 tablespoon of the filling in the centre of the circle. Pinch the edges of the wrapper together to enclose the filling and form a tight ball.
6 Fill a wok or saucepan one third full of water and bring to the boil. Put the dumplings in a bamboo steamer lined with baking paper, leaving a gap between each one. Cover and steam for 7–8 minutes. Serve with chilli sauce.

NOTE: Wheat starch is a very fine white powder similar to cornflour. Available at Asian food stores.

Use lightly oiled hands to roll the dough into a ball.

Roll out the small pieces of dough into flat rounds.

Pinch the edges of the wrapper together so that the filling is enclosed.

MACADAMIA-CRUSTED CHICKEN STRIPS WITH MANGO SALSA

Preparation time: 25 minutes +
   30 minutes refrigeration
Cooking time: 15 minutes
Makes 24

12 chicken tenderloins (700 g), larger
   ones cut in half
seasoned plain flour, for dusting
2 eggs, lightly beaten
250 g macadamias, finely chopped
2 cups (160 g) fresh breadcrumbs
oil, for deep-frying

Mango salsa
1 small mango, very finely diced
2 tablespoons finely diced red onion
2 tablespoons roughly chopped fresh
   coriander leaves
1 fresh green chilli, seeded and finely
   chopped
1 tablespoon lime juice

1 Cut the chicken into strips. First, dust the chicken strips with the flour, then dip them in the egg and, finally, coat them in the combined nuts and breadcrumbs. Refrigerate for at least 30 minutes to firm up.
2 To make the salsa, combine all the ingredients in a small bowl and season to taste with salt and pepper.
3 Fill a large heavy-based saucepan or deep-fryer one third full of oil and heat to 180°C (350°F), or until a cube of bread dropped in the oil

browns in 15 seconds. Cook the chicken in batches for 2–3 minutes, or until golden brown all over, taking care not to burn the nuts. Drain on crumpled paper towels. Serve warm with the salsa.

THINK AHEAD: These are best made on the day they are to be served.
VARIATIONS: The chicken strips are also very tasty served with sweet chilli sauce. Try a different coating using almonds or peanuts.

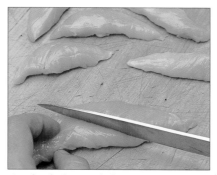

Cut the chicken tenderloins into even bite-size strips.

Using your hands, coat the chicken strips in the macadamia crumbs.

VIETNAMESE RICE PAPER ROLLS

Preparation time: 1 hour 10 minutes +
    10 minutes soaking
Cooking time: Nil
Makes 48

Nuoc cham dipping sauce
¾ cup (185 ml) fish sauce
¼ cup (60 ml) lime juice
2 tablespoons grated palm sugar
    or soft brown sugar
2 bird's eye chillies, seeded
    and finely chopped

150 g dried rice vermicelli
48 round 15 cm rice paper wrappers
48 cooked king prawns, peeled,
    deveined and halved lengthways
150 g bean sprouts
3 cups (60 g) fresh mint
2 cups (60 g) fresh coriander leaves

1 To make the dipping sauce, combine all the ingredients and ½ cup (125 ml) water and stir until the sugar dissolves. Transfer to two small serving dishes and set aside.
2 Place the noodles in a heatproof bowl, cover with boiling water and soak for 10 minutes, then drain.
3 Assemble the rolls one at a time. Dip a rice paper wrapper in a bowl of warm water for 30 seconds, or until it softens. Place the wrapper on a work surface and put 2 prawn halves on the bottom third of the wrapper. Top with a few noodles, bean sprouts, 3 mint leaves and 6 coriander leaves, in that order. Ensure that the filling is neat and compact, then turn up the bottom of the wrapper to cover the filling. Holding the filling in place, fold in the two sides, then roll up.
4 Arrange on a platter, folded-side-down. Cover with a damp tea towel or plastic wrap until ready to serve. Serve with the dipping sauce.

THINK AHEAD: You can make the rolls up to 8 hours beforehand, but make sure you cover them well or they will dry out rapidly. The sauce can be made a day early.

Put the filling ingredients on the bottom third of the rice paper wrapper.

Fold up the bottom of the wrapper, then the sides before rolling up the wrapper.

CARAMELISED RED ONION AND FETA TARTLETS

Preparation time: 20 minutes
Cooking time: 45 minutes
Makes 24

1½ tablespoons olive oil
2 large red onions, finely chopped
2 teaspoons chopped fresh thyme
3 sheets ready-rolled shortcrust
 pastry
70 g feta, crumbled
2 eggs, lightly beaten
½ cup (125 ml) cream

1 Preheat the oven to moderate 180°C (350°F/Gas 4). Heat the oil in a frying pan (do not use a non-stick one or the onion won't caramelise). Add the onion and cook, stirring occasionally, over medium–low heat for 30 minutes, or until dark gold. Add the thyme, stir well and transfer to a bowl to cool.
2 Grease 24 shallow patty tin holes. Using an 8 cm cutter, cut out 24 pastry rounds and line the tins with the rounds.
3 Divide the onion among the patty cases, then spoon the feta over the onion. Combine the eggs with the cream, season and pour into the pastry cases. Bake for 10–15 minutes, or until puffed and golden. Leave in the tins for 5 minutes before transferring to a wire rack to cool.

THINK AHEAD: These can be made a day in advance and reheated in a slow (150°C/300°F/Gas 2) oven for

10 minutes before serving.
VARIATION: For creamy herb tartlets, follow the method outlined for the tartlets above and use the following filling. Mix together 2 beaten eggs, 2 tablespoons milk, ½ cup (125 ml) cream, 2 teaspoons

chopped fresh chives and 1 teaspoon each of chopped fresh dill, thyme and parsley. Pour into the pastry cases and sprinkle with grated Parmesan, using only about 2 tablespoons all together. Bake for 10–15 minutes, or until puffed and golden.

Stir the onion occasionally until it is dark golden and caramelised.

Cut out 24 pastry rounds and use to line the patty tins.

Pour the creamy filling into each of the pastry cases.

SCALLOPS ON POTATO CRISPS WITH PEA PUREE

Preparation time: 45 minutes
Cooking time: 30 minutes
Makes 48

1 tablespoon butter
3 French shallots, finely chopped
1 clove garlic, finely chopped
2 slices mild pancetta, finely chopped
1 cup (155 g) frozen peas
¼ cup (60 ml) chicken stock or water
oil, for deep-frying, plus 1 tablespoon
4–5 floury potatoes (e.g. russet, King Edward), peeled and very thinly sliced to get 48 slices

24 scallops, cut in half horizontally through the centre
fresh mint, to garnish

1 Melt the butter in a small saucepan and fry the shallots, garlic and pancetta over low heat for 3 minutes, or until soft but not coloured. Add the peas and stock, and cook over high heat for 3 minutes, or until all the liquid has evaporated. Cool a little, transfer to a food processor and purée until smooth. Season.
2 Fill a deep heavy-based saucepan or deep-fryer one third full of oil and heat to 190°C (375°F), or until a cube of bread dropped into the oil browns in 10 seconds. Cook the potato slices in batches until crisp and golden. Drain on crumpled paper towels and sprinkle with salt.
3 Toss the scallops with 1 tablespoon oil. Season lightly. Heat a chargrill pan to hot, then sear the scallops in batches for 5 seconds each side, or until lightly browned on the outside but opaque in the middle.
4 Reheat the pea purée. Dollop 1 teaspoon of purée on each potato crisp, then top with a scallop. Season with pepper and garnish with mint.

THINK AHEAD: The purée can be made 2 days early and refrigerated. The crisps can be cooked 2 hours early; store in an airtight container.

Cook the shallots, garlic, pancetta, peas and stock until the liquid evaporates.

Cook the potato slices in hot oil until they are golden and crispy.

Sear the scallops a few at a time until they are lightly browned.

47

HONEY MUSTARD CHICKEN DRUMETTES

Preparation time: 20 minutes +
2 hours marinating
Cooking time: 45 minutes
Makes 24

1/3 cup (80 ml) oil
1/4 cup (90 g) honey
1/4 cup (60 ml) soy sauce
1/4 cup (60 g) Dijon mustard
1/4 cup (60 ml) lemon juice
4 cloves garlic, crushed
24 chicken drumettes (see Note)

1 To make the marinade, place the oil, honey, soy sauce, mustard, lemon juice and garlic in a large non-metallic dish and mix together thoroughly.
2 Trim the chicken of excess fat, then place in the dish with the marinade and toss until well coated.

Cover and refrigerate for at least 2 hours, or preferably overnight, turning 2–3 times.
3 Preheat the oven to moderately hot 200°C (400°F/Gas 6). Place the drumettes on a wire rack over a foil-lined baking tray. Bake, turning and brushing with the marinade 3–4 times, for 45 minutes, or until golden brown and cooked. Serve immediately with serviettes for sticky fingers.

NOTE: Drumettes are the chicken wing with the wing tip removed.
THINK AHEAD: Cook a day ahead and reheat in a warm (160°C/315°F/ Gas 2–3) oven for 10–12 minutes.
VARIATION: For a teriyaki marinade, combine 1/2 cup (125 ml) teriyaki sauce, 1/4 cup (60 ml) pineapple juice, 2 tablespoons honey, 1 tablespoon grated fresh ginger, 2 cloves crushed garlic and 1 teaspoon sesame oil in a bowl.

Trim the excess fat from the chicken drumettes.

Lay the chicken on a wire rack over a foil-lined baking tray to catch the drips.

TURKISH BREAD WITH HERBED ZUCCHINI

Preparation time: 15 minutes
Cooking time: 35 minutes
Makes 48

½ large loaf Turkish bread
1 tablespoon sesame seeds
½ cup (125 ml) vegetable oil

Herbed zucchini
1 tablespoon olive oil
2 cloves garlic, finely chopped
4 x 100 g small zucchini, roughly chopped
1 large carrot, thinly sliced
2 tablespoons chopped fresh flat-leaf parsley
2 tablespoons chopped fresh mint
2 teaspoons lemon juice
½ teaspoon ground cumin

1 Split the bread horizontally through the middle and open it out. Cut the bread into 3 cm squares; you should end up with 48 squares.

2 Toast the sesame seeds in a large dry non-stick frying pan over low heat for 2–3 minutes, or until golden. Remove from the pan. Heat the vegetable oil in the same pan and cook the bread in batches for 1–2 minutes each side, or until crisp and golden. Drain on paper towels.
3 Heat the olive oil in a saucepan over medium heat and cook the garlic for 1 minute. Add the zucchini and carrot and cook over medium heat for 2 minutes. Season with salt and pepper. Add 1 tablespoon water, cover and simmer over low heat for

15 minutes, or until the vegetables are soft. Spoon into a bowl and mash roughly with a potato masher. Add the parsley, mint, lemon juice and cumin. Season to taste.
4 Spoon 2 teaspoons of the zucchini mixture over each square of bread and scatter with sesame seeds. Serve warm or at room temperature.

THINK AHEAD: The herbed zucchini can be prepared up to 2 days in advance. Reheat just before serving.

Split the bread in half horizontally, then cut it into 3 cm squares.

Use a potato masher to mash the zucchini and carrot mixture.

variations on a theme STICKS

These are perfect for an outdoor party or a casual gathering. If you are using bamboo skewers, soak them in cold water for 30 minutes before using so they don't catch alight.

SESAME BEEF SKEWERS
Ready in under an hour

1/2 cup (125 ml) soy sauce
1/3 cup (80 ml) Chinese rice wine
2 cloves garlic, crushed
1 teaspoon finely grated fresh ginger
1 teaspoon sesame oil
225 g scotch fillet, cut into 2 cm
 cubes
8 spring onions
2 tablespoons toasted sesame seeds

Combine the soy sauce, wine, garlic, ginger and oil, and pour over the beef. Marinate for 20 minutes. Drain, reserving the marinade.

Cut six of the spring onions into 24 x 3 cm pieces and thread a piece plus two meat cubes onto 24 skewers. Cook on a hot barbecue hotplate or chargrill pan for 5 minutes, or until cooked. Remove, sprinkle with sesame seeds and keep warm.

Put the reserved marinade in a saucepan and bring to the boil for 1 minute, then add 2 thinly sliced spring onions. Pour into a bowl and serve with the skewers. Makes 24.

SATAY CHICKEN STICKS
Ready in 1 hour 15 minutes

8 large chicken tenderloins, trimmed
 and sliced into thirds lengthways
1 clove garlic, crushed
3 teaspoons fish sauce
2 teaspoons grated fresh ginger
24 kaffir lime leaves
lime quarters, to serve

Satay sauce
2 teaspoons peanut oil
4 red Asian shallots, finely chopped
2 cloves garlic, chopped
2 teaspoons grated fresh ginger
2 small fresh red chillies, finely
 chopped
200 ml coconut milk
1/2 cup (125 g) crunchy peanut butter
2 tablespoons grated palm sugar or
 soft brown sugar
2 tablespoons lime juice
1 1/2 tablespoons fish sauce
2 teaspoons soy sauce
1 fresh kaffir lime leaf

Combine the chicken, garlic, fish sauce and ginger. Cover, then refrigerate for 1 hour.

To make the sauce, heat the oil in a saucepan over medium heat. Add the shallots, garlic, ginger and chilli and cook for 5 minutes, or until golden. Add the rest of the ingredients, reduce the heat and simmer for 10 minutes, or until thick.

Thread a lime leaf and a chicken strip onto each skewer, then cook on a hot barbecue hotplate or chargrill pan for 3–4 minutes. Serve with satay sauce and lime wedges. Makes 24.

LEMON GRASS PRAWNS
Ready in under an hour

6 lemon grass stems, cut in half
    lengthways, then in half crossways
1 kg peeled and deveined prawns
3 spring onions, roughly chopped
4 tablespoons fresh coriander leaves
2 tablespoons fresh mint
2 tablespoons fish sauce
1½ tablespoons lime juice
1–2 tablespoons sweet chilli sauce,
    plus extra for serving
peanut oil, for brushing

Soak the lemon grass in water for
30 minutes, then pat dry. Process the
prawns, spring onion, coriander, mint,
fish sauce, lime juice and chilli sauce
in a food processor. Take a tablespoon
of the mix and mould around the end
of a lemon grass stem, using wet hands.
Refrigerate for 30 minutes.

    Brush a barbecue hotplate or
chargrill pan with the oil. Cook the
skewers, turning occasionally, for
5 minutes, or until cooked. Serve
with sweet chilli sauce. Makes 24.

CHARGRILLED VEGETABLE SKEWERS
Ready in under an hour

24 bay leaves
12 button mushrooms, cut in half
1 yellow capsicum, cut into 2 cm
    pieces
1 red capsicum, cut into 2 cm pieces
1 zucchini, cut into 2 cm pieces
1 small red onion, cut into 2 cm
    pieces
½ cup (125 ml) olive oil
2 tablespoons lemon juice
1 clove garlic, crushed
2 teaspoons fresh thyme

Concassé

1 tablespoon olive oil, extra
1 small onion, finely chopped
1 clove garlic, crushed
425 g can chopped tomatoes
4 tablespoons torn fresh basil

Thread 24 skewers in the following
order: bay leaf, mushroom, yellow
capsicum, red capsicum, zucchini
and onion, then put in a large flat
non-metallic dish and season with
salt and cracked black pepper.

    Place the oil, lemon juice, garlic
and thyme in a small bowl and mix
together. Pour over the skewers and
marinate for 20 minutes.

    Meanwhile, to make the concassé,
heat the extra oil in a small saucepan,
add the onion and cook for 5 minutes,
or until soft. Add the garlic and cook
for 30 seconds, then add the tomato.
Simmer for 10–15 minutes over
medium heat, then add the basil.
Cook the skewers on a hot barbecue
hotplate or chargrill pan for 3 minutes
each side, or until golden, brushing
occasionally with the marinade. Serve
with the concassé. Makes 24.

*From left: Sesame beef skewers, Satay
chicken sticks, Lemon grass prawns,
Chargrilled vegetable skewers.*

ROSTI WITH SMOKED TROUT AND SALSA VERDE

Preparation time: 15 minutes
Cooking time: 30 minutes
Makes 32

1 small smoked trout
450 g floury potatoes (e.g. russet,
    King Edward or pontiac)
2 spring onions, thinly sliced
1/3 cup (80 ml) olive oil

Salsa verde
1 1/2 cups (30 g) fresh flat-leaf parsley
1 cup (30 g) fresh basil
1 tablespoon capers, drained
1 tablespoon chopped gherkin or
    4 cornichons (baby gherkins)
2 anchovies, drained
1 clove garlic, chopped
2 teaspoons Dijon mustard
1/4 cup (60 ml) olive oil
1 tablespoon lemon juice

1 Remove the skin from the trout, pull the flesh from the bones and flake into pieces.

2 To make the salsa verde, place the parsley, basil, capers, gherkin, anchovies, garlic and mustard in a food processor and blend until finely chopped. While the motor is running, blend in the oil and lemon juice until mixed together. Season with pepper.

3 To make the rösti, peel and coarsely grate the potatoes. Squeeze out as much liquid as possible. Put the flesh in a bowl with the spring onion and mix together. Heat the oil in a large heavy-based frying pan over medium–high heat. To cook the rösti, take heaped teaspoons of the potato mixture, add to the pan in batches and press down with an egg flip to help the potato stay together. Cook for 2–3 minutes each side, or until crisp and golden. Drain on crumpled paper towels.

4 Top each rösti with a teaspoon of salsa verde then some flakes of trout. Serve warm or at room temperature.

THINK AHEAD: The rösti can be made 8 hours beforehand and kept in an airtight container lined with paper towels. Reheat for 5 minutes in a moderate (180°C/350°F/Gas 4) oven.

Remove the flesh from the smoked trout, being careful to throw out any bones.

Blend the salsa verde ingredients together until they are finely chopped.

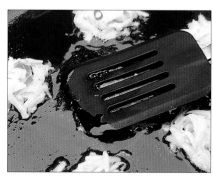

Cook the rösti in batches, slightly flattening each one with an egg flip.

CHICKEN LIVER PARFAIT

Preparation time: 45 minutes +
    4 hours refrigeration
Cooking time: 20 minutes
Makes 48

35 g butter
2 French shallots, peeled and sliced
500 g chicken livers, any fatty white
    tissue removed
¼ cup (60 ml) thick cream
1 tablespoon cognac or brandy
48 Melba toasts
8 cornichons (baby gherkins), thinly
    sliced on the diagonal

1 Heat a large frying pan over
medium heat. Melt the butter, then
add the shallots to the pan and cook,
stirring, for 4–5 minutes, or until
they are soft and transparent. Using
a slotted spoon transfer them to a
food processor.
2 In the same pan, add the chicken
livers and cook in batches over high
heat, stirring, for 4–5 minutes, or
until seared on the outside but still
pink and quite soft on the inside.
Add to the food processor along with
2 tablespoons of the pan juices, the
cream, cognac and some salt and
pepper. Blend for 4–5 minutes, or
until quite smooth. Push through a
fine sieve to remove any remaining
lumps. Transfer to a bowl or serving
dish, put plastic wrap directly
on the surface of the mixture and
refrigerate for at least 4 hours, or
until cold.
3 To serve, spoon a heaped teaspoon
of parfait onto each Melba toast
and top with a slice of cornichon.
Alternatively, leave the parfait in the
serving dish, supply a small knife and
allow guests to help themselves.

THINK AHEAD: The parfait can be
made up to 3 days in advance and
stored in the fridge in an airtight
container. Assemble no more than
30 minutes before serving.
VARIATION: For a really sumptuous
and indulgent treat, substitute duck
livers for the chicken livers in the
parfait. The flavour will be much
richer and well worth the extra cost
for a special occasion. Cook the duck
livers exactly the same way as the
chicken livers.

Cook the French shallots in the butter,
stirring regularly.

Blend the chicken livers with the other
ingredients until quite smooth.

QUAIL EGGS WITH SPICED SALTS

Preparation time: 20 minutes
Cooking time: 5 minutes
Makes 48

2 teaspoons cumin seeds
48 quail eggs
½ cup (125 g) good-quality table salt
1½ teaspoons Chinese five-spice powder
3 teaspoons celery salt

1 Toast the cumin seeds in a dry frying pan over low heat for 1–2 minutes, or until richly fragrant. Cool slightly, then grind until finely crushed into a powder.
2 Place half the eggs in a large saucepan of water, bring to the boil and cook for 1½ minutes for medium–hard boiled eggs. Remove from the pan and rinse under cold water to cool. Repeat with the remaining eggs. Peel when cold—this is easiest done under gently running cold water.
3 Divide the table salt among three small bowls and add the Chinese five-spice powder to one, the celery salt to another and the ground cumin to the third. Mix the flavourings into the salt in each bowl.

4 To serve, pile the eggs into a large bowl and serve each of the salts in a small bowl. Invite your guests to dip their egg into the flavoured salt of their choice.

THINK AHEAD: The eggs can be prepared the day before they are to be served and the spiced salts can be made up to 2 weeks earlier and stored in airtight containers.

Crush the cumin seeds into a fine powder with a mortar and pestle.

Carefully place half the quail eggs in a saucepan of water.

ROAST VEGETABLE AND GOAT'S CHEESE ROULADE

Preparation time: 1 hour +
  2 hours refrigeration
Cooking time: 30 minutes
Makes 48

Pesto
2 cups (60 g) fresh basil
30 g pine nuts, toasted
1 clove garlic
50 ml olive oil
1/4 cup (25 g) finely grated Parmesan

4 red capsicums
1 eggplant, sliced lengthways into
  5 mm slices
1/4 cup (60 ml) olive oil, plus extra
  for brushing
100 g soft goat's cheese, lightly
  beaten until smooth
15 large fresh basil leaves
1 loaf olive bread, crusts removed
  and cut into 5 mm thick slices

1 To make the pesto, place the basil, pine nuts and garlic in a food processor and process until finely chopped. With the motor running, add the olive oil in a thin stream until well combined. Transfer to a bowl, add the Parmesan, season and mix well. Place plastic wrap directly onto the surface of the pesto and refrigerate until needed.

2 Cut the capsicums into halves, removing the seeds and membrane. Place, skin-side-up, under a hot grill and cook for 10 minutes, or until the skin blackens and blisters. Place in a plastic bag, leave to cool, then peel away the skin, leaving the capsicum as intact as possible. Trim the ends so that the pieces are even and flat.

3 Brush the eggplant slices with olive oil and cook on a very hot chargrill pan for 3–5 minutes each side, or until cooked.

4 To assemble sprinkle a flat work surface with water and place a 50 cm long piece of plastic wrap on top (the water helps secure the plastic). Lay half the capsicum strips on the plastic

to form a rectangle 30 cm x 13 cm. Lightly season the capsicum. Layer half the eggplant over the capsicum, then spread with half the cheese to cover the entire rectangle. Season. Lay half the basil leaves in a single layer over the cheese. Using the plastic wrap, tightly roll up the capsicum lengthways, sealing the ends. Wrap tightly in foil and twist the ends firmly. Repeat with the remaining ingredients to make another roll, then refrigerate for at least 2 hours.

5 Preheat the oven to moderate 180°C (350°F/Gas 4). Stamp out 48 rounds from the olive bread using a cutter the same width as the roulade, ideally 4 cm diameter. Brush the rounds lightly with olive oil and bake for 5–10 minutes, or until crisp and lightly browned. Spread 1/2 teaspoon of pesto on each croûton. Remove the plastic from the roulade and, using a very sharp knife, slice into 5 mm thick slices and place one slice on each croûton.

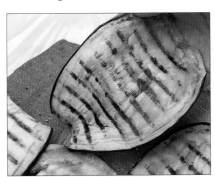

Lay the strips of chargrilled eggplant over the capsicum slices.

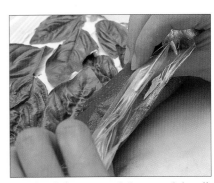

Use the plastic wrap to help you tightly roll up the vegetables.

THAI FISH CAKES WITH DIPPING SAUCE

Preparation time: 25 minutes
Cooking time: 15 minutes
Makes 24

500 g firm white fish fillets, skin removed
1½ tablespoons red curry paste
¼ cup (60 g) sugar
¼ cup (60 ml) fish sauce
1 egg
100 g snake beans, thinly sliced
10 fresh kaffir lime leaves, finely chopped
oil, for deep-frying

Dipping sauce

½ cup (125 g) sugar
¼ cup (60 ml) white vinegar
1 tablespoon fish sauce
1 small fresh red chilli, chopped
2 tablespoons finely chopped carrot
2 tablespoons peeled, seeded and finely chopped cucumber
1 tablespoon roasted peanuts, chopped

1 Place the fish in a food processor and process until smooth. Add the curry paste, sugar, fish sauce and egg. Process for another 10 seconds, or until combined. Stir in the beans and chopped lime leaves.

2 Shape the mixture into walnut-size balls, then flatten them into patties.

3 Fill a wok one third full of oil and heat to 180°C (350°F), or until a cube of bread dropped into the oil browns in 15 seconds. Cook in batches for 3–5 minutes, turning occasionally. Drain on crumpled paper towels.

4 To make the dipping sauce, place the sugar, vinegar, fish sauce, chilli and ½ cup (125 ml) water in a saucepan. Simmer for 5 minutes, or until thickened slightly. Cool. Stir in the chopped carrot, cucumber and peanuts. Serve the dipping sauce with the fish cakes.

THINK AHEAD: The fish cakes can be prepared, shaped and placed on baking trays lined with plastic wrap and kept in the fridge a day ahead. Cook them just before serving.

Slice the snake beans very thinly using a sharp knife.

Process the fish cake mixture until it is well combined.

Shape walnut-sized amounts of mixture into mini patties.

POLENTA WEDGES WITH BOCCONCINI AND TOMATO

Preparation time: 30 minutes +
  1 hour setting
Cooking time: 40 minutes
Makes 48

1 tablespoon olive oil
1²/3 cups (250 g) polenta
³/4 cup (75 g) grated Parmesan
2¹/2 tablespoons ready-made or
  home-made pesto from page 55
150 g bocconcini, thinly sliced
12 cherry tomatoes, cut into quarters
¹/2 cup (15 g) fresh basil, larger
  leaves torn

1 Lightly grease a 20 cm x 30 cm baking tin with the olive oil. Bring 1 litre lightly salted water to the boil in a saucepan. Once the water is boiling, add the polenta in a steady stream, stirring continuously to prevent lumps forming. Reduce the heat to very low and simmer, stirring regularly, for about 20–25 minutes, or until the polenta starts to come away from the side of the pan.
2 Stir the Parmesan into the polenta and season with salt and pepper. Spoon the polenta into the baking tray, smooth the top with the back of a wet spoon and leave for 1 hour, or until set.
3 Once the polenta has set, carefully tip it out onto a board and cut into 24 x 5 cm squares, then cut each square into two triangles. Chargrill the polenta in batches on a preheated chargrill pan for 2–3 minutes on each side, or until warmed through.
4 Spread each triangle with 1 teaspoon of the pesto, top with a slice of bocconcini and a tomato quarter. Season and grill for 1–2 minutes, or until the cheese is just starting to melt. Garnish with basil and serve immediately.

THINK AHEAD: The polenta can be made up to 3 days ahead. Assemble up to 2 hours before serving, then grill at the last moment.

Add a steady stream of the polenta to the boiling water.

Stir the grated Parmesan into the cooked polenta.

Chargrill the wedges of polenta until they are warmed through.

variations on a theme MINI PIZZAS

The first step to making these mini pizzas is to make the dough for the bases. Next, make your topping, assemble and pop in the oven for a few minutes. Voilà! You have 24 tasty pizzas.

BASIC PIZZA DOUGH

7 g sachet dried yeast
1/2 teaspoon caster sugar
2 cups (250 g) plain flour
1 tablespoon olive oil

Mix the yeast, sugar and 3/4 cup (185 ml) warm water in a small bowl, then cover and set aside for 10 minutes, or until frothy. If it hasn't foamed after 10 minutes, discard it and start again.

Sift the flour and 1/2 teaspoon salt into a large bowl and make a well in the centre. Pour in the yeast mixture and add the oil. Mix with a flat-bladed knife, using a cutting action, until a dough forms. Turn out onto a lightly floured work surface and knead for 10 minutes, or until smooth. Transfer to a large lightly oiled bowl, cover with plastic wrap and leave for 45 minutes, or

until it has doubled in size.

Preheat the oven to very hot 230°C (450°F/Gas 8). Punch down the dough, then knead for 8 minutes, or until elastic. Divide the dough into 24 equal portions and roll each portion into a ball with your hands. Working in batches, use a rolling pin to roll each ball into a circle 3–4 mm thick and 4.5 cm in diameter. Prick the surfaces a few times with a fork and brush with oil. Keep any unrolled balls covered so that they do not dry out while you are working.

Place the rounds on a lightly greased baking tray, top with the filling of your choice and bake for 8–10 minutes. Makes 24.

NOTE: If you are making the Turkish pizza, you will need 1 1/2 quantities of the dough; for the others, you will only need 1 quantity.

PRAWN AND PESTO

Ready in under 3 hours

2 tablespoons olive oil
1 teaspoon finely chopped fresh basil
1 clove garlic, crushed
24 cooked medium prawns, peeled and deveined
1/4 cup (60 g) ready-made or home-made pesto from page 55
24 pizza dough bases
24 small fresh basil leaves
24 pine nuts

Combine the oil, chopped basil, garlic and prawns in a non-metallic bowl. Cover with plastic wrap and refrigerate for 30 minutes. Spread a level 1/2 teaspoon of pesto over each pizza dough base, leaving a narrow border. Put a prawn, basil leaf and pine nut in the middle of each pizza, then cook.

TANDOORI CHICKEN
Ready in under 3 hours

1/4 cup (60 g) ready-made tandoori
   paste
1 clove garlic, crushed
4 tablespoons chopped fresh
   coriander leaves, plus extra for
   garnish
1/2 cup (125 g) plain yoghurt
550 g chicken thigh fillets, trimmed
   and cut into small dice
1 small cucumber, peeled, halved,
   seeds removed and chopped
1 tablespoon oil, plus extra for drizzling
2 teaspoons plain yoghurt, extra
24 pizza dough bases

Combine the tandoori paste, garlic,
3 tablespoons of the coriander, and
1/4 cup (60 g) yoghurt in a non-metallic
bowl. Toss the chicken in the mixture,
then cover and refrigerate.

Meanwhile, put the cucumber in a
sieve. Sprinkle with salt and leave for
30 minutes. Rinse, squeeze dry and
combine with the remaining yoghurt
and coriander. Refrigerate until needed.

Heat the oil in a large frying pan
and cook the chicken in batches over
medium–high heat for 6–8 minutes,
or until tender. Stir in the extra
yoghurt. Spoon a heaped teaspoon of
chicken on each base and flatten with
the back of the spoon. Drizzle with
oil. Cook, then top with cucumber
mix and garnish with coriander.

TURKISH PIZZA
Ready in under 3 hours

1 tablespoon olive oil, plus extra for
   brushing
375 g lamb mince
1 onion, finely chopped
1/4 cup (40 g) pine nuts
1 tomato, peeled, seeded and chopped
1/4 teaspoon ground cinnamon
pinch allspice
2 teaspoons chopped fresh coriander,
   plus extra for serving
2 teaspoons lemon juice
1 1/2 quantities pizza dough
1/4 cup (60 g) plain yoghurt

Heat the oil in a frying pan over
medium heat and cook the mince for
3 minutes, or until it browns. Add
the onion and cook over low heat for
6–8 minutes, or until soft. Add the
pine nuts, tomato, spices, 1/4 teaspoon
cracked black pepper and some salt
and cook for 8 minutes, or until dry.
Stir in the coriander and lemon juice
and season.

Roll the pizza dough into 24 ovals.
Spoon some filling onto the centre of
each base. Draw up and pinch
together the two short sides to form a
boat shape, then brush with oil. Cook.
Spoon 1/2 teaspoon yoghurt on each
pizza, then scatter with coriander.

*From left: Prawn and pesto, Tandoori
chicken, Turkish pizza.*

VEGETABLE PAKORAS WITH MINTED YOGHURT SAUCE

Preparation time: 20 minutes
Cooking time: 35 minutes
Makes 40

1 cup (250 g) plain yoghurt
1 cup (20 g) fresh mint
2 tablespoons coriander seeds
1 tablespoon cumin seeds
1½ cups (165 g) besan (chickpea
    flour) (see Note)
1½ teaspoons chilli powder
1 teaspoon ground turmeric
3 tablespoons finely chopped fresh
    coriander
1 teaspoon oil
400 g cauliflower florets, cut into
    1 cm pieces
1 small onion, thinly sliced
1 cup (135 g) grated zucchini
1 clove garlic, crushed
oil, for deep-frying
lemon wedges, to serve

1 To make the dipping sauce, put the yoghurt and mint in a food processor and pulse for 10–20 seconds, or until the mint is thoroughly chopped.
2 Toast the coriander and cumin seeds in a dry frying pan over low heat for 2–3 minutes, or until fragrant. Cool slightly, then grind to a powder. Transfer to a large bowl and add the besan, chilli powder, turmeric, fresh coriander and 1 teaspoon salt. Mix well, stir in the oil, then gradually add ⅔ cup (170 ml) warm water and stir until a smooth, thick paste forms.
3 Mix the cauliflower, onion, zucchini and garlic into the batter.
4 Fill a deep heavy-based saucepan or deep-fryer one third full of oil and heat to 180°C (350°F), or until a cube of bread dropped into the oil browns in 15 seconds. Carefully add 1 tablespoon of the pakora mixture to the oil, then repeat until you are cooking five pakoras at one time. Cook each batch for 2 minutes each side, or until golden. Drain on crumpled paper towels. Sprinkle with salt and repeat with the remaining mixture. Serve hot with yoghurt sauce and lemon wedges.

NOTE: Besan flour is available from health food stores.
THINK AHEAD: The yoghurt sauce will keep for 2 days. The batter and vegetables should be combined and cooked just before serving.

Process the mint and yoghurt until the mint is thoroughly chopped.

Add the vegetables to the batter and keep stirring until well mixed.

GOAT'S CHEESE, WALNUT AND BEETROOT CREPE ROLLS

Preparation time: 20 minutes +
  30 minutes standing
Cooking time: 1 hour 50 minutes
Makes 48

2 small or 1 medium beetroot
2 cloves garlic, unpeeled
1 teaspoon olive oil
1 cup (125 g) plain flour
2 eggs
1½ cups (375 ml) milk
30 g butter, melted and cooled
1 cup (100 g) walnut halves
40 g butter, extra
150 g soft goat's cheese
48 fresh basil leaves

1 Preheat the oven to moderately hot 200°C (400°F/Gas 6). Scrub the beetroot clean. Sit the beetroot and garlic on a piece of foil, add the oil, season with salt and pepper, then wrap up in the foil. Place on a baking tray and roast for 1–1¼ hours, or until tender. Remove from the oven, and when cool enough to handle, peel the skin from the beetroot and garlic. Place the flesh in a food processor and blend until finely chopped. Reduce the oven to moderate 180°C (350°F/Gas 4).
2 Sift the flour into a large bowl and make a well in the centre. Gradually add the combined eggs, milk and melted butter, whisking to a smooth batter. Add the beetroot mixture, cover and leave for 30 minutes.
3 Spread the walnuts on a baking tray and roast for 5–10 minutes, or until lightly golden. Finely chop.
4 Transfer the beetroot mixture to a jug for easier pouring. Melt 1 teaspoon of the extra butter in a crepe pan or frying pan. Pour one eighth of the mixture into the pan, shaking the pan gently to spread the mixture out thinly. Cook for 1–2 minutes, or until bubbles appear around the edges. Flip gently with a palette knife or spatula and cook the other side for 1 minute, or until just

set. Transfer to a plate and repeat with the remaining ingredients to make eight crepes.
5 Beat the goat's cheese in a bowl until smooth. Season to taste.
6 Lay one crepe out on a work surface and gently spread it with one eighth of the cheese. Sprinkle with one eighth of the walnuts and 6 basil leaves. Roll up gently, but firmly, then

repeat with the remaining ingredients to make eight rolls. Remove the ends and slice each roll into six 2 cm slices.

THINK AHEAD: The crepes can be made up to 2 days in advance. Store in the fridge with a piece of plastic wrap between each one. Assemble up to 2 hours before serving and keep in the fridge until ready to serve.

When the beetroot and garlic are cool enough to touch, peel off the skins.

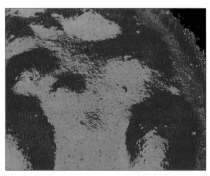

Cook the beetroot batter until bubbles start to appear around the edges.

CRUNCHY THAI CHICKEN AND PEANUT CAKES

Preparation time: 15 minutes +
    30 minutes refrigeration
Cooking time: 15 minutes
Makes 24

3 teaspoons grated palm sugar
    or soft brown sugar
1 tablespoon fish sauce
350 g chicken mince
3/4 cup (120 g) toasted peanuts,
    chopped
1/2 cup (40 g) fresh breadcrumbs
1 tablespoon red Thai curry paste
1 tablespoon lime juice

3 fresh kaffir lime leaves, very finely
    shredded
2 tablespoons sweet chilli sauce
2 tablespoons chopped fresh
    coriander
1/2 cup (125 ml) oil
1 banana leaf, cut into 24 x 5 cm
    square pieces
sweet chilli sauce, extra, to serve

1 Dissolve the sugar in the fish sauce, then place in a large bowl with the chicken mince, peanuts, breadcrumbs, curry paste, lime juice, lime leaves, sweet chilli sauce and coriander. Mix well. Divide the mixture into 24 small balls—they will be quite soft. Flatten the balls

into discs about 1.5 cm thick. Lay them in a single layer on a tray, cover with plastic wrap and refrigerate for 30 minutes.
2 Heat the oil in a heavy-based frying pan and cook the cakes in batches for 2–3 minutes each side, or until firm and golden. Drain on crumpled paper towels.
3 Place a chicken cake on each square of banana leaf and top with a dash of sweet chilli sauce. Secure with a toothpick for easier serving.

THINK AHEAD: The uncooked Thai chicken cakes will keep frozen for up to 2 months or refrigerated in a single layer for 1 day.

Finely shred the kaffir lime leaves with a sharp knife.

Combine all the ingredients for the Thai cakes in a large bowl.

Cook the Thai chicken cakes until they are golden brown and feel firm.

SPRING ROLLS

Preparation time: 45 minutes +
    45 minutes standing
Cooking time: 20 minutes
Makes 30

2 dried shiitake mushrooms
250 g pork mince
1½ tablespoons dark soy sauce
2 teaspoons dry sherry
½ teaspoon five-spice powder
2 tablespoons cornflour, plus
    1½ teaspoons
⅓ cup (80 ml) peanut oil
½ celery stick, finely chopped
2 spring onions, thinly sliced
30 g drained bamboo shoots,
    cut into matchsticks
¾ cup (40 g) shredded Chinese
    cabbage
2 cloves garlic, crushed
2 teaspoons finely chopped fresh
    ginger
¼ teaspoon sugar
¼ teaspoon sesame oil
250 g packet 12 cm square spring
    roll wrappers
oil, for deep-frying

Dipping sauce
2 tablespoons soy sauce
1 tablespoon hoisin sauce
1 tablespoon plum sauce
1 tablespoon sweet chilli sauce

1 Soak the mushrooms in ½ cup
(125 ml) warm water for 30 minutes.
Drain, discard the stalks and thinly
slice the caps.
2 Mix the mince, soy sauce, sherry,
five-spice powder and 1 tablespoon
of the cornflour in a non-metallic
bowl. Leave for 15 minutes.
3 Heat 2 tablespoons of the peanut
oil in a wok over high heat until
nearly smoking, then cook the celery,
spring onion, bamboo shoots and
cabbage for 3–4 minutes, or until just
soft. Add some salt, then remove
from the wok.
4 Heat the remaining peanut oil in
the wok and cook the garlic and
ginger for 30 seconds. Add the pork
mixture and stir-fry for 2–3 minutes,

or until the mince is nearly cooked.
Combine 1½ teaspoons of the
cornflour with ¼ cup (60 ml) water.
Return the cooked vegetables to the
wok, then stir in the mushrooms. Add
the sugar, sesame oil and cornflour
mixture and stir for 2 minutes.
Remove from the heat and cool.
5 To make the dipping sauce, mix all
the ingredients and ⅓ cup (80 ml)
water in a bowl.
6 Make a paste with the remaining
cornflour and 2–3 teaspoons cold
water. To wrap the spring rolls, place
a wrapper on a workbench with one
corner pointing towards you. Put
2 teaspoons of the filling in the

centre, then brush the edges with
a little cornflour paste. Roll up,
tucking in the sides as you do so.
Continue with the remaining filling
and wrappers.
7 Fill a heavy-based saucepan or
wok one third full of oil and heat to
180°C (350°F), or until a cube of
bread dropped into the oil browns in
15 seconds. Deep-fry the spring rolls
in batches until golden brown, then
drain on crumpled paper towels.
Serve hot with the dipping sauce.

THINK AHEAD: Spring rolls can be
frozen for up to 2 months prior to
cooking. Thaw before deep-frying.

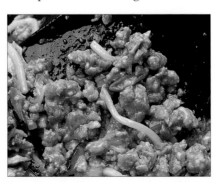

*Toss the pork mixture constantly until it is
nearly cooked.*

*Fold in the bottom then the two sides of the
wrappers before folding up.*

MEDITERRANEAN TWISTS

Preparation time: 15 minutes
Cooking time: 35 minutes
Makes 24

2 tablespoons olive oil
2 onions, thinly sliced
1/3 cup (80 ml) dry white wine
3 teaspoons sugar
1 cup (30 g) chopped fresh flat-leaf
    parsley
8 anchovies, drained and finely
    chopped
1 cup (130 g) coarsely grated Gruyère
    cheese
6 sheets filo pastry
60 g unsalted butter, melted

1 Preheat the oven to hot 220°C (425°F/Gas 7) and warm a baking tray. Heat the oil in a frying pan and cook the onion over low heat for 5 minutes. Add the wine and sugar, and cook for 10–15 minutes, or until the onion is golden. Remove from the heat and cool.
2 Combine the parsley with the anchovies, cheese and cooled onion.
3 Keeping the filo covered while you work, take one sheet, brush lightly with the butter, cover with another sheet and repeat until you have three buttered sheets. Spread the parsley mixture over the pastry and top with the remaining three sheets, buttering each layer as before. Press down firmly, then cut the pastry in half widthways, then cut each half into strips 1.5–2 cm wide. Brush with butter, then gently twist each strip. Lightly season with black pepper,

place on a baking tray and bake for 10–15 minutes, or until golden.

THINK AHEAD: Make the twists up to 2 days before the party and store them in an airtight container. To refresh them, warm them in a moderate (180°C/350°F/Gas 4) oven

for 10 minutes before serving.
VARIATION: There are many variations to these twists, but a great one to try is Parmesan and thyme twists. Simply substitute the Gruyère with 3/4 cup (75 g) coarsely grated Parmesan and replace the parsley with 2 teaspoons of thyme.

Cook the onion with the wine and sugar until it is soft and golden.

Spread the parsley mixture over the sheets of filo pastry.

Use a ruler to help you cut thin strips from the pastry.

ASPARAGUS AND PROSCIUTTO BUNDLES WITH HOLLANDAISE

Preparation time: 10 minutes
Cooking time: 15 minutes
Makes 24

24 spears fresh asparagus, trimmed
8 slices prosciutto, cut into thirds lengthways

Hollandaise
175 g butter
4 egg yolks
1 tablespoon lemon juice
ground white pepper

1 Blanch the asparagus in boiling salted water for 2 minutes, then drain and refresh in cold water. Pat dry, then cut the spears in half. Lay the bottom half of each spear next to its tip, then secure together by wrapping a piece of prosciutto around them.

2 To make the hollandaise, melt the butter in a small saucepan. Skim any froth off the top. Cool the butter a little. Combine the egg yolks and 2 tablespoons of water in a small heatproof bowl placed over a saucepan of simmering water, making sure the base of the bowl does not touch the water. Using a wire whisk, beat for about 3–4 minutes, or until the mixture is thick and foamy. Make sure the bowl does not get too hot or you will end up with scrambled eggs. Add the butter slowly, a little at a time at first, whisking well between each addition. Keep adding the butter in a thin stream, whisking continuously, until all the butter has been used. Try to avoid using the milky whey in the bottom of the pan, but don't worry if a little gets in. Stir in the lemon juice and season with salt and white pepper. Place in a bowl and serve warm with the asparagus.

THINK AHEAD: Hollandaise can be made 1 day in advance and stored, covered, in the fridge. To reheat, put the bowl over a saucepan of simmering water, making sure it does not touch the water, and whisk until just warm.

Briefly cook the asparagus in boiling water, then drain.

Wrap the tip and bottom end of each spear in a piece of prosciutto.

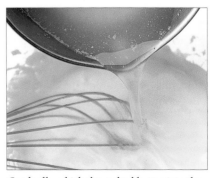

Gradually whisk the melted butter into the hollandaise mixture.

SANDWICHES

At first, sandwiches might not seem like an exciting option for a party, but think again. These miniature versions of your favourites will be a big hit.

MINI STEAK SANDWICHES
Ready in under 1 hour

100 ml olive oil
1 onion, thinly sliced
3/4 cup (15 g) fresh parsley
10 large fresh basil leaves
20 fresh mint leaves
1 clove garlic, crushed
1 tablespoon Dijon mustard
1 tablespoon capers
2 anchovy fillets
400 g fillet steak, about 1 cm thick
1 baguette, cut into 40 x 5 mm slices

Heat 2 tablespoons of oil in a frying pan and cook the onion over low heat for 25 minutes, or until caramelised.

To make the salsa verde, place the parsley, basil, mint, garlic, mustard, capers, anchovies and the remaining oil in a food processor and pulse to a thick paste. Season.

Cut out 20 rounds from the steak with a 2.5 cm cutter. Season, then sear on a lightly oiled chargrill pan on both sides for 1–2 minutes, or until cooked to your liking. Put a little of the onion on 20 rounds of bread, top with a piece of steak and a dollop of salsa verde, then top with the remaining bread. Serve warm. Makes 20.

MINI FOCACCIA WITH ROASTED VEGETABLES
Ready in under 1 hour

2 red capsicums
2 yellow capsicums
3 slender eggplants
2 large zucchini
1 red onion
1/3 cup (80 ml) extra virgin olive oil
3 cloves garlic, crushed
12 mini focaccias, halved
1/4 cup (60 g) ready-made or
    home-made pesto from page 55
3 large bocconcini, sliced

Preheat the oven to moderately hot 200°C (400°F/Gas 6). Cut the red and yellow capsicums into 3 cm pieces. Slice the eggplants and zucchini into 1 cm rounds, then thinly slice the onion. Place all the vegetables in a roasting tin with the oil and garlic, then season with salt and cracked black pepper and toss together thoroughly. Roast for 25 minutes, or until cooked.

Spread each half of the focaccia with 1/2 teaspoon of the pesto and divide the vegetables among them. Place two slices of bocconcini on top of each base, then top with the lid. Toast the focaccias on both sides on a hot chargrill pan until heated through.

Slice each focaccia in half, then wrap a 3 cm wide band of double greaseproof paper around the middle of the sandwiches and secure with string. Serve warm. Makes 24.

SMOKED TROUT TEA SANDWICHES
Ready in about 30 minutes

24 thin slices brown bread
softened cream cheese, to spread
1 large telegraph cucumber, cut into
    wafer-thin slices
400 g good-quality smoked trout
2 tablespoons roughly chopped
    fresh dill
lemon wedges, to garnish

Spread the bread with cream cheese. Lay a single layer of cucumber on half the bread slices. Layer the trout on top of the cucumber, then place the other bread slices on top. Cut off the crusts, then slice into four triangles. Place the sandwiches long-edge-down on a platter to form a pyramid. Brush one side of the pyramid with softened cream cheese, then sprinkle with dill. Garnish with lemon. Makes 48.

PETIT CROQUE-MONSIEUR
Ready in about 30 minutes

1 loaf of bread, sliced into 6 slices
    lengthways (see Note)
1/2 cup (125 g) wholegrain mustard
100 g thinly shaved honey ham
100 g thinly sliced Jarlsberg cheese
1/3 cup (55 g) very finely chopped
    mustard fruits (optional)
40 g butter
2 tablespoons olive oil

Brush each slice of bread with 1 tablespoon of mustard. Divide the ham and cheese into three portions and lay one portion of the ham, then the cheese, on three bread slices. If you are using mustard fruits, sprinkle them over the cheese. Press the other bread slices, mustard-side-down, on top so that you have three large sandwiches. Cut eight rounds from each sandwich with a 5 cm cutter. Melt half the butter and oil in a non-stick frying pan and, when the butter begins to foam, cook half the rounds until crisp and golden and the cheese is just starting to melt. Keep warm on a baking tray in a warm oven while you cook the remaining rounds. Serve warm. Makes 24.

NOTE: Either ask your baker to slice the bread lengthways or buy an unsliced loaf and do it yourself.
VARIATION: To transform the croque-monsieur to a croque-madame, fry 24 quail eggs in a little oil and butter. Then, stamp a neat circle out of the egg with a 5 cm cutter. Place an egg on top of each sandwich.

From left: Mini steak sandwiches, Mini focaccia with roasted vegetables, Smoked trout tea sandwiches, Petit croque-monsieur.

PRAWN TOASTS

Preparation time: 20 minutes
Cooking time: 15 minutes
Makes 36

Dipping sauce
½ cup (125 ml) tomato sauce
2 cloves garlic, crushed
2 small fresh red chillies, seeded and
    finely chopped
2 tablespoons hoisin sauce
2 teaspoons Worcestershire sauce

350 g raw medium prawns
1 clove garlic
75 g canned water chestnuts, drained
1 tablespoon chopped fresh coriander
2 cm x 2 cm piece fresh ginger,
    roughly chopped
2 eggs, separated
¼ teaspoon white pepper
12 slices white bread, crusts removed
1 cup (155 g) sesame seeds
oil, for deep-frying

1 To make the dipping sauce, combine all the ingredients in a small bowl.
2 Peel the prawns and gently pull out the dark vein from each prawn back, starting at the head end. Put the prawns in a food processor with the garlic, water chestnuts, coriander, ginger, egg whites, pepper and ¼ teaspoon salt and process for 20–30 seconds, or until smooth.
3 Brush the top of each slice of bread with lightly beaten egg yolk, then spread evenly with the prawn mixture. Sprinkle generously with sesame seeds. Cut each slice of bread into three even strips.

4 Fill a large heavy-based saucepan or deep-fryer one third full of oil and heat to 180°C (350°F), or until a cube of bread dropped into the oil browns in 15 seconds. Deep-fry the toasts in small batches for 10–15 seconds, or until golden and crisp. Start with the prawn mixture face down, then turn halfway through.

Remove the toasts from the oil with tongs or a slotted spoon and drain on crumpled paper towels. Serve with the dipping sauce.

THINK AHEAD: The uncooked prawn toasts can be frozen for up to 1 month. Allow them to thaw slightly before deep-frying as instructed.

Pull the dark vein out of the prawns from the head end.

Use a food processor to blend the prawn mixture until it is smooth.

Brush the bread with egg yolk, then spread with the prawn mixture.

MONEY BAGS

Preparation time: 40 minutes
Cooking time: 20 minutes
Makes 30

1 tablespoon peanut oil
4 red Asian shallots, finely chopped
(see Note)
2 cloves garlic, crushed
1 tablespoon grated fresh ginger
150 g chicken mince
150 g pork mince
¼ cup (40 g) roasted peanuts,
chopped
3 tablespoons finely chopped
fresh coriander leaves
3 teaspoons fish sauce
2 teaspoons soy sauce
2 teaspoons lime juice
2 teaspoons grated palm sugar or
soft brown sugar
30 won ton wrappers
oil, for deep-frying
garlic chives, for tying

Dipping sauce
2 teaspoons sugar
½ cup (125 ml) vinegar
2 small fresh red chillies, seeded and
chopped

1 Heat the oil in a frying pan over medium heat. Add the shallots, garlic and ginger and cook for 1–2 minutes, or until the shallots are soft. Add the mince and cook for 4 minutes, or until cooked, breaking up any lumps with the back of a wooden spoon. Stir in the peanuts, coriander, fish sauce, soy sauce, lime juice and sugar and cook, stirring, for 1–2 minutes, or until mixed and reduced. Cool.

2 Form your thumb and index finger into a circle, then place a won ton wrapper on top of the circle. Place 2 teaspoons of the cooled mixture in the centre, then lightly brush the edges with water. Push the mixture down firmly with your free hand, tightening the circle of your thumb and index finger at the same time, making a smaller circle and encasing the mixture firmly in the wrapper and forming a 'bag'. Trim the edges.

3 Fill a deep heavy-based saucepan or deep-fryer one third full of oil and heat to 190°C (375°F), or until a cube of bread dropped in the oil browns in 10 seconds. Cook in batches for 30–60 seconds, or until golden. Drain. Tie the 'neck' of the money bags with the chives.

4 To make the dipping sauce, dissolve the sugar and 1 teaspoon salt in the vinegar. Add the chilli and mix together. Serve the money bags with the dipping sauce.

NOTE: Red Asian shallots are small onions. If you can't find them, use one small red onion instead.

Cook the mince, breaking up any lumps with the back of a wooden spoon.

Put 2 teaspoons of the filling in the centre of the won ton wrapper.

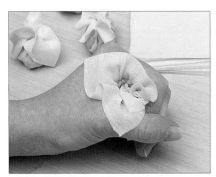

Tighten the circle of your thumb and finger until the mixture is encased in a 'bag'.

OLIVE AND POTATO BALLS WITH PESTO

Preparation time: 20 minutes +
  30 minutes refrigeration
Cooking time: 30 minutes
Makes 30

650 g floury potatoes (e.g. russet,
  King Edward)
1 tablespoon olive oil
1 onion, finely chopped
2 cloves garlic, finely chopped
1/2 cup (80 g) pitted Kalamata olives,
  sliced
1/3 cup (40 g) plain flour
1/4 cup (25 g) grated Parmesan
1/4 cup (15 g) shredded fresh basil
1 egg
3/4 cup (45 g) dry Japanese
  breadcrumbs
oil, for deep-frying
1/4 cup (60 g) ready-made or
  home-made pesto from page 55
2 slices prosciutto, sliced into thin
  strips

1 Cut the potatoes into 4 cm chunks and steam or boil for 15 minutes, or until tender. Drain well, then mash with a potato masher.
2 Heat the olive oil in a frying pan and cook the onion over medium heat for 4–5 minutes, or until soft. Add the garlic and cook for an extra minute. Remove from the heat, cool and add to the potato. Mix in the olives, flour, Parmesan, basil and egg, and a little salt and cracked black pepper. Shape the mixture into 30 small balls, then refrigerate for 30 minutes. Roll the balls in breadcrumbs, pressing the breadcrumbs on firmly so that the balls are evenly coated.
3 Fill a deep heavy-based saucepan or deep-fryer one third full of oil and heat to 180°C (350°F), or until a cube of bread dropped in the oil browns in 15 seconds. Cook the olive and potato balls in batches for 2–3 minutes, or until golden. Drain on crumpled paper towels. Top each one with 1/2 teaspoon of the pesto and a piece of prosciutto.

NOTE: The mixture is a little soft, but cooks up well, giving a smooth texture. The Japanese breadcrumbs provide a good crisp coating, but you can also use normal breadcrumbs.
THINK AHEAD: The balls can be frozen for up to 2 months before cooking or refrigerated for 2 days.

Mix the rest of the ingredients into the mashed potato.

Once the balls have firmed in the refrigerator, roll them in the breadcrumbs.

ZUCCHINI AND HALOUMI FRITTERS

Preparation time: 15 minutes
Cooking time: 25 minutes
Makes 45

300 g zucchini
4 spring onions, thinly sliced
200 g haloumi cheese, coarsely grated
1/4 cup (30 g) plain flour
2 eggs
1 tablespoon chopped fresh dill, plus sprigs, to garnish
1/4 cup (60 ml) oil
1 lemon, cut into very thin slices, seeds removed
1/3 cup (90 g) thick Greek-style yoghurt

1 Coarsely grate the zucchini and squeeze out as much liquid as possible in your hands or in a clean tea towel. Combine the zucchini with the spring onion, haloumi, flour, eggs and dill. Season well with salt and cracked black pepper.

2 Heat the oil in a large heavy-based frying pan. Form fritters (using heaped teaspoons of the mixture) and cook in batches for 2 minutes each side, or until golden and firm. Drain on crumpled paper towels.

3 Cut each slice of lemon into quarters or eighths, depending on the size, to make small triangles.

4 Top each fritter with 1/2 teaspoon yoghurt, a piece of lemon and a small sprig of dill.

NOTE: The fritters are best prepared and cooked as close to the serving time as possible or the haloumi tends to go a little tough.

Squeeze as much liquid as possible from the grated zucchini.

Cook the fritters until they are nicely golden on both sides.

71

DRESSED-UP BABY POTATOES

Preparation time: 25 minutes
Cooking time: 45 minutes
Makes 24

24 even bite-sized new potatoes,
    washed and dried
1/3 cup (80 ml) olive oil
1 tablespoon drained capers,
    patted dry
1 rasher bacon
1 tablespoon cream
10 g butter
1/2 cup (125 g) sour cream
1 tablespoon chopped fresh chives
1 tablespoon red or black caviar

1 Preheat the oven to moderate 180°C (350°F/Gas 4). Line a baking tray with baking paper. Place the potatoes in a bowl and toss with half the olive oil. Sprinkle with salt and black pepper, then put on the baking tray and bake for 40 minutes, or until cooked through, rotating them 2–3 times so that they brown evenly.
2 Meanwhile, heat the remaining oil in a frying pan and cook the capers over high heat, or until they open into small flowers. Drain on paper towels. Cook the bacon under a hot grill until crispy. Cool, then finely chop.
3 Remove the potatoes from the oven. When cool enough to handle, cut a thin lid from each potato. Discard the lids. Use a melon baller or small teaspoon to scoop out the flesh from the middle of the potatoes, leaving a 1 cm border. Put the potato flesh in a bowl and mash thoroughly with the cream, butter and salt and black pepper. Spoon the mash back into the potatoes.
4 Top each potato with a small dollop of sour cream. Divide the potatoes into four groups of six and use a separate topping for each group: capers, bacon, chives and caviar.

THINK AHEAD: The potatoes can be pre-prepared up to the filled with mash stage. Reheat, covered, in a warm (160°C/315°F/Gas 2–3) oven for 10 minutes, cool slightly, then add the toppings.

Turn the potatoes once or twice during cooking so they brown evenly.

Once the capers have opened into small flowers, drain them on paper towels.

Scoop out a small amount of flesh from the potatoes, reserving the flesh.

MINI CRAB CAKES WITH CORIANDER PASTE

Preparation time: 35 minutes +
    30 minutes refrigeration
Cooking time: 20 minutes
Makes 24

1 tablespoon butter
4 spring onions, thinly sliced
1 egg
2 tablespoons sour cream
350 g fresh white crab meat, excess
    liquid squeezed out
1 small yellow capsicum, finely diced
2 teaspoons chopped fresh thyme
2½ cups (200 g) fresh white
    breadcrumbs
olive oil, for shallow-frying

Coriander paste
1 clove garlic
1 green chilli, seeded
½ teaspoon ground cumin
¼ teaspoon sugar
¾ cup (25 g) fresh coriander leaves
½ cup (10 g) fresh mint
1 tablespoon lemon juice
25 ml coconut cream
½ avocado

1 Line a tray with baking paper. Melt the butter in a frying pan over low heat. When it begins to foam, add the spring onion and cook for 1–2 minutes, or until softened. Remove from the heat and cool.
2 Place the egg and sour cream in a bowl and mix until just smooth. Add the cooled spring onion, crab meat, capsicum, thyme and ½ cup (40 g) of the breadcrumbs, season and mix together. Shape the mixture into flat rounds, using 1 level tablespoon of the mixture for each round. Place each one on the lined tray and refrigerate for 30 minutes.
3 Meanwhile, to make the coriander paste, place the garlic, chilli, cumin, sugar, herbs, lemon juice and ¼ teaspoon salt in a food processor until a fine paste forms. Add the coconut cream and continue to blend until smooth. Add the avocado and, using the pulse action, process until

just smooth. Transfer to a small bowl, cover with plastic wrap and refrigerate.
4 Put the remaining breadcrumbs in a bowl and coat the crab cakes, one at a time, using your hands to ensure that the breadcrumbs have stuck.
5 Heat enough olive oil in a non-stick frying pan to just coat the bottom. Cook the crab cakes in batches for 2–3 minutes each side, or until golden. Drain on crumpled paper

Form the crab mixture into mini patties with your hands.

towels and serve warm with ½ teaspoon of coriander paste on each one.

THINK AHEAD: You can pan-fry the crab cakes a day early and refrigerate. To reheat, warm them on a baking tray in a moderate (180°C/350°F/ Gas 4) oven for 6–8 minutes. Or, you can freeze the uncooked patties in single layers for up to 2 months.

Blend the coriander paste in the food processor until it is smooth.

variations on a theme SUSHI

To make successful sushi, you must first make special sushi rice, then assemble the sushi. Sushi is best eaten within a few hours of being made because refrigeration will dry it out.

BASIC SUSHI RICE
2½ cups (550 g) white sushi rice
  (see Note)
100 ml rice vinegar
2 tablespoons sugar
1 tablespoon mirin

Rinse the rice under cold running water until the water runs clear, then sit it in a strainer for 1 hour to drain.

Transfer to a large saucepan with 3 cups (750 ml) water, bring to the boil and cook, without stirring, for 5–10 minutes, or until tunnels start to form on the surface. Reduce the heat to low, cover and cook for 12–15 minutes, or until tender. Remove from the heat, remove the lid from the pan, cover with a clean tea towel and leave for 15 minutes.

To make the dressing for the rice, combine the vinegar, sugar, mirin and 1 teaspoon salt in a bowl and stir until the sugar dissolves.

Spread the rice over a flat non-metallic tray, pour the dressing on top and mix with a spatula. Gently separate the grains of rice. Spread out the rice and cool to body temperature —if it gets too cold, it will turn hard and be difficult to work with. Spread a damp tea towel over the rice and keep it covered as you work. To prevent any rice from sticking to your hands, dip them in a bowl of warm water with a few drops of rice vinegar in it. Makes 6 cups.

NOTE: In Japan they use Japonica rice to make sushi rice. Rice for making sushi is available from Asian food stores.

MAKI ZUSHI
Ready in under 3 hours

250 g sashimi tuna
1 small Lebanese cucumber
½ avocado
8 sheets nori
½ quantity prepared sushi rice
3 teaspoons wasabi paste

Cut the tuna, cucumber and avocado into thin strips. Place a sheet of nori on a bamboo mat, shiny-side-down, with a short end towards you. (Bamboo mats are available at Asian grocery stores. There isn't really a substitute if you want to make successful sushi.) Spread the rice about 1 cm thick over the nori, leaving a 1 cm border. Make a shallow groove down the centre of the rice towards the short end closest to you. Spread a small amount of wasabi along the groove. Place a

selection of strips of your filling ingredients on top of the wasabi. Lift up the edge of the bamboo mat and roll the sushi, starting from the edge nearest to you. When you've finished rolling, press the mat to make either a round or square roll. Push in any rice that is escaping from the ends. Wet a sharp knife, trim the ends and cut the roll in half and then each half into three. Repeat. Makes 48.

LAYERED SUSHI
Ready in under 4 hours

1/3 cup (90 g) Japanese mayonnaise
2 teaspoons wasabi paste
4 sheets nori
1 quantity prepared sushi rice
300 g smoked salmon
1/4 cup (40 g) pickled ginger slices
black sesame seeds, to garnish

Combine the mayonnaise and wasabi in a small bowl. Lay a sheet of nori, shiny-side-up, on top of a piece of baking paper on a dry tray. Entirely cover the nori with a loosely packed cup of rice. Spread with wasabi mayonnaise, then top with a layer of smoked salmon and some slices of pickled ginger. Place another sheet of nori on top and flatten lightly with a rolling pin. Repeat the layering twice, to form three layers, finishing with a sheet of nori, and again flattening with the rolling pin. Reserve the remaining wasabi mayonnaise.

Cover and refrigerate for at least an hour, then, using a very sharp knife dipped in water, trim any filling protruding from the edges and slice into 2 cm squares. Garnish with wasabi mayonnaise, pickled ginger and black sesame seeds. Makes 36.

NIGIRI ZUSHI
Ready in under 3 hours

250 g sashimi tuna or salmon
lemon juice
1 quantity prepared sushi rice
2 teaspoons wasabi paste
1 sheet nori, cut into strips

Use a sharp knife to trim the fish into a neat rectangle, then cut into paper-thin slices, cleaning your knife in a bowl of water and lemon juice after cutting each slice. Form a tablespoon of sushi rice into an oval about the same size as your pieces of fish. Place a piece of fish on the open palm of your left hand, then spread a small dab of wasabi over the centre. Place the rice on the fish and gently cup your palm to make a curve. Using the middle and index fingers of your right hand, press the rice onto the fish, firmly pushing with a slight downward motion to make a neat shape. Turn over and repeat the shaping process, finishing with the fish on top of the rice. Tie a strip of nori around the centre of each one. Makes 16–20.

From left: Maki zushi, Layered sushi, Nigiri zushi.

SPRING ONION PANCAKES WITH CHINESE BARBECUE PORK

Preparation time: 35 minutes +
  30 minutes resting time
Cooking time: 15 minutes
Makes 24

Spring onion pancakes
1 cup (125 g) plain flour
2 teaspoons oil
100 ml boiling water
1½ teaspoons sesame oil
2 spring onions, thinly sliced
oil, for pan-frying

Topping
1 tablespoon oil
175 g Chinese barbecue pork,
  cut into 24 slices
1 clove garlic, crushed
2 tablespoons hoisin sauce
1 teaspoon oyster sauce
1 teaspoon soy sauce
1 teaspoon sugar
½ teaspoon sesame oil
1 teaspoon cornflour
fresh coriander sprigs, to garnish

1 Sift the flour and ¼ teaspoon salt into a bowl, make a well in the centre and add the oil and boiling water. Stir well until the mixture is moistened and a soft dough forms. Turn onto a floured board and knead for 5 minutes until the dough is smooth and elastic. Use more flour if necessary to prevent the dough sticking. Cover the dough with a tea towel and rest for 15 minutes.
2 Roll the dough into a long sausage shape, then cut into 24 pieces. Shape each piece into a ball, then flatten into a 5–6 cm round. Brush each round with sesame oil and sprinkle with the chopped spring onion. Roll the pancakes like a Swiss roll, then flatten with your hands. Roll again from the other side, then shape into a 4 cm round. Stack the pancakes on baking paper and rest for 15 minutes.
3 To make the topping, heat the oil in a wok or frying pan and stir-fry the pork for about a minute, then add the

garlic and toss for 30 seconds. Add the hoisin, oyster sauce, soy sauce, sugar and sesame oil. Make a paste by mixing the cornflour with ½ cup (125 ml) cold water, then pour into the wok and stir for 1–2 minutes, or until the sauce boils and thickens. Remove from the wok.
4 Pour 1 cm of oil into a frying pan and heat to 180°C (350°F), or until a cube of bread dropped in the oil sizzles. Cook the pancakes in batches for 1–2 minutes each side, or until golden brown. Remove from the pan and drain on crumpled paper towels.

5 To serve, place 1 slice of the pork topping onto each pancake and garnish with a sprig of coriander. Serve warm.

NOTE: Chinese barbecue pork is pork that is coated in a thick sweet glaze before cooking. It can be bought from Chinese barbecue shops.
THINK AHEAD: You can make the pancakes up to 2 days in advance and store them in the fridge. To reheat, place the pancakes in a moderate (180°C/350°F/Gas 4) oven for 5–8 minutes, or until crisp.

Sprinkle the dough rounds with spring onion, then roll them up.

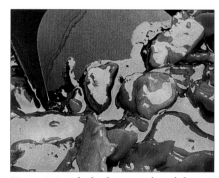

Keep stirring the barbecue pork and the sauce until the sauce thickens.

wasabi powder and black sesame seeds to the bowl and toss until the tuna cubes are evenly coated.

3 Heat a wok over high heat, add half the oil and swirl to coat. Add half the tuna and cook, tossing gently, for 1–2 minutes, or until lightly golden on the outside but still pink in the middle. Drain on crumpled paper towels and repeat with the remaining oil and tuna. Arrange on a platter with dipping sauce in the centre and serve with toothpicks so that your guests can pick up the cubes.

THINK AHEAD: The dipping sauce will keep in the refrigerator for up to 1 week, but the tuna is best if cooked no more than 3 hours in advance.
VARIATION: The tuna cubes are also very nice served with a Chilli and lime dipping sauce instead of the Ginger and soy one in the recipe. To make the dipping sauce, dissolve 2 tablespoons grated palm sugar or soft brown sugar in a small bowl with 2 tablespoons lime juice. Add 1 tablespoon fish sauce and 1 seeded and finely chopped fresh red bird's eye chilli. Mix together well. This sauce will keep in the refrigerator for 2–3 days.

SESAME AND WASABI-CRUSTED TUNA CUBES

Preparation time: 10 minutes
Cooking time: 5 minutes
Makes about 40 cubes

Ginger and soy dipping sauce
2 cm x 2 cm piece fresh ginger, cut into julienne strips
2 tablespoons Japanese soy sauce
2 tablespoons mirin
1 teaspoon wasabi paste
¼ teaspoon sesame oil

Tuna cubes
600 g fresh tuna steaks
1 teaspoon wasabi powder
⅓ cup (50 g) black sesame seeds
¼ cup (60 ml) oil
toothpicks, for serving

1 To make the dipping sauce, place the ginger, Japanese soy sauce, mirin, wasabi paste and sesame oil in a small bowl and mix together well. Set aside until needed.

2 Cut the tuna into 2 cm cubes using a very sharp knife. Put the tuna cubes in a bowl. Add the combined

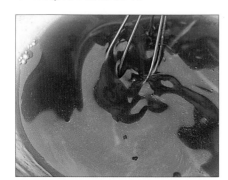

Mix all the dipping sauce ingredients together in a small bowl.

Use a sharp knife to cut the tuna steaks into even 2 cm cubes.

Coat the tuna cubes in the black sesame seeds and wasabi powder.

77

MINI ROASTED VEGETABLE FRITTATAS

Preparation time: 30 minutes
Cooking time: 40 minutes
Makes 48

1/3 cup (80 ml) olive oil
3 French shallots, thinly sliced
3 cloves garlic, crushed
4 slender eggplants, sliced
    lengthways into 5 mm slices
2 zucchinis, sliced lengthways into
    5 mm slices
2 red capsicums, seeded and cut
    into 2–3 flat pieces
2 tablespoons finely chopped fresh
    mint
1/2 cup (15 g) fresh basil, torn into
    small pieces
8 eggs
1/2 cup (125 ml) cream
pinch of ground nutmeg
1/4 cup (25 g) grated Parmesan
fresh parsley, to garnish

1 Preheat the oven to moderately hot 200°C (400°F/Gas 6). Lightly grease 48 non-stick mini muffin holes. Heat the oil, shallots and garlic together in a small saucepan over low heat for 1–2 minutes, or until just soft. Remove from the heat.
2 Place the eggplant and zucchini slices in a single layer on a baking tray and brush on both sides with the hot oil. Roast the vegetables for about 10 minutes, then turn and cook for another 10 minutes, or until golden.
3 Meanwhile, place the capsicum strips, skin-side-up, under a hot grill until the skin blackens and blisters. Cool in a plastic bag, then peel away the skin. Cut into 2 cm x 1 cm strips, then transfer to a bowl.
4 Remove the vegetables from the oven. Reduce the temperature to moderate 180°C (350°F/Gas 4). Slice the vegetables into 2 cm x 1 cm strips and add to the bowl. Add the herbs, season and mix well.
5 Beat the eggs, cream, nutmeg and Parmesan together in a large bowl and season with salt and pepper.
6 Fill each muffin hole a third full with assorted pieces of vegetable mixture. Carefully pour the egg mixture in just short of the top. Distribute the remaining vegetables among the holes, pressing the pieces into the egg. Use the remaining egg mixture to top up the levels to equal heights. Place a small piece of parsley leaf on top of each. Transfer to the oven and bake for about 15 minutes, or until golden and set. The frittatas will rise a lot while cooking, but will sink once out of the oven. Cool for 5 minutes before turning out onto a wire rack. Serve warm or cold.

THINK AHEAD: These frittatas can be made 2 days early and refrigerated in an airtight container. Bring to room temperature before serving.

Brush the zucchini slices with a little of the hot oil.

Pour the egg mixture into the muffin holes, stopping just before reaching the top.

GOAT'S CHEESE FRITTERS WITH ROASTED CAPSICUM SAUCE

Preparation time: 20 minutes +
   30 minutes refrigeration
Cooking time: 30 minutes
Makes 30

Roasted capsicum sauce
2 red capsicums
2 tablespoons olive oil
1 small red onion, finely chopped
1 clove garlic
1/3 cup (80 ml) chicken or vegetable
   stock

420 g ricotta, well drained
400 g goat's cheese, crumbled
2 tablespoons chopped fresh chives
1/4 cup (30 g) flour
2 eggs, lightly beaten
1 cup (100 g) dry breadcrumbs
oil, for deep-frying

1 Cut the capsicums into 2–3 pieces, removing the seeds and membrane. Place, skin-side-up, under a hot grill until the skin blackens and blisters. Cool in a plastic bag, then peel away the skin and roughly chop the flesh.
2 Heat the olive oil in a frying pan over medium heat and cook the onion and garlic for 4–5 minutes, or until softened. Add the capsicum and stock. Bring to the boil, then remove from the heat, cool slightly and transfer to a food processor. Pulse until combined, but still a little lumpy. Season to taste with salt and cracked black pepper and refrigerate until needed.
3 Combine the ricotta, goat's cheese and chives in a bowl. Add the flour and eggs, then season and mix well.
4 Put the breadcrumbs in a bowl. Roll a level tablespoon of the cheese mixture into a ball with damp hands, then flatten slightly and coat in the breadcrumbs. Repeat with the remaining mixture. Refrigerate for 30 minutes.
5 Fill a deep heavy-based saucepan or deep-fryer one third full of oil and heat to 180°C (350°F), or until a

cube of bread browns in 15 seconds. Cook the fritters in batches for 1 minute, or until browned, then remove from the pan and drain on crumpled paper towels. Serve warm with the roasted capsicum sauce.

THINK AHEAD: The uncooked fritters can be frozen for up to 2 months or refrigerated for 2 days. The roasted capsicum sauce can be made up to 5 days in advance and kept in the refrigerator until needed.

Using a pulse action, process the capsicum mixture until well combined.

Cover all of the fritters with an even coating of breadcrumbs.

LAMB KORMA ON MINI POPPADOMS

Preparation time: 15 minutes +
  2 hours marinating
Cooking time: 15 minutes
Makes 24

350 g lamb backstrap, cut into
  1.5 cm cubes
2 tablespoons korma curry paste
1 clove garlic, crushed
1 teaspoon ground coriander
1/2 cup (125 g) thick natural yoghurt
oil, for deep-frying
24 round 4 cm poppadoms (chilli
  flavour, if available)
1 tablespoon oil, extra
1 1/2 tablespoons mango chutney
small fresh coriander leaves, to
  garnish

1 Place the lamb, curry paste, garlic, ground coriander and half the yoghurt in a non-metallic bowl and stir until well combined. Cover and marinate in the refrigerator for 1–2 hours.

2 Meanwhile, fill a deep heavy-based saucepan or deep-fryer one third full of oil and heat to 180°C (350°F), or until a cube of bread dropped into the oil browns in 15 seconds. Cook the poppadoms a few at a time for a few seconds each, or until they are puffed and lightly golden. Remove with a slotted spoon and drain on crumpled paper towels.

3 Heat a wok over high heat, add the extra oil and swirl to coat. Add the marinated lamb and cook in batches, stirring, for 4–5 minutes, or until the lamb is cooked through. Spoon a heaped teaspoon onto each poppadom and top with 1/2 teaspoon of the remaining yoghurt, then 1/4 teaspoon of the chutney. Garnish with a coriander leaf and serve immediately.

THINK AHEAD: Lamb korma can be cooked and frozen for up to 2 months, or refrigerated for 2–3 days. Reheat in a saucepan over low heat until warm.
VARIATIONS: You can make chicken korma instead, by replacing the lamb with 350 g diced chicken tenderloins.

If you can't find the 4 cm poppadoms, use the normal-size ones and break them into pieces.

Use a sharp knife to cut the lamb into even-sized cubes.

Cook the poppadoms in the hot oil until golden, then remove with a slotted spoon.

VEGETABLE SAMOSAS

Preparation time: 35 minutes +
   cooling
Cooking time: 45 minutes
Makes 45

2 tablespoons ghee or oil
1 small onion, diced
1 tablespoon hot curry paste
200 g potatoes, cut into 1 cm cubes
150 g orange sweet potato, peeled
   and cut into 1 cm cubes
1 tablespoon soft brown sugar
½ cup (80 g) frozen peas
⅓ cup (50 g) salted roasted cashew
   nuts, chopped
½ cup (25 g) roughly chopped fresh
   coriander leaves
1 kg (5 sheets) bought shortcrust
   pastry
oil, for deep-frying

Dipping sauce
2 cups (500 g) thick Greek-style
   yoghurt
1 cup (30 g) fresh coriander leaves,
   roughly chopped
1 teaspoon ground cumin

1 Heat the ghee in a large heavy-based saucepan over medium heat. Cook the onion and curry paste for 5–6 minutes, stirring regularly until fragrant and the onion is golden.
2 Add the potato, orange sweet potato and sugar and stir well. Cook, stirring regularly, for 8–10 minutes, or until the potatoes are just tender. Stir in the frozen peas, reduce the heat to low, cover and cook for a further 5 minutes; if the mixture is sticking, add 1–2 tablespoons of water. Transfer to a bowl and cool to room temperature.
3 To make the dipping sauce, put all the ingredients in a small bowl and mix together well. Refrigerate until needed.
4 Season the cooled vegetable mixture with salt and pepper, then add the cashews and coriander.
5 Using a 7 cm cutter, cut nine circles from each sheet of pastry. Place 1 rounded teaspoon of filling in the middle of each circle. Fold the pastry over to completely encase the filling and gently pinch the sides together, forming a half moon.
6 Fill a deep heavy-based saucepan or deep-fryer one third full of oil and heat to 170°C (325°F), or until a cube of bread dropped in the oil browns in approximately 20 seconds. Deep-fry 4–5 samosas at a time for 3 minutes, or until crisp and the pastry has 'blistered' a little. Remove with a slotted spoon and drain on crumpled paper towels. Serve warm with the dipping sauce.

THINK AHEAD: The samosas can be assembled, then frozen in a single layer for up to 2 months. Thaw them before deep-frying.

Stir the potato and sweet potato cubes into the curry mixture.

Place a heaped teaspoon of filling in the centre of each pastry circle.

MINI HAMBURGERS

Preparation time: 30 minutes
Cooking time: 10 minutes
Makes 24

8 burger buns, split in half (see Note)
400 g beef mince
¼ cup (25 g) dry breadcrumbs
3 French shallots, very finely chopped
1 tablespoon Dijon mustard
1 tablespoon Worcestershire sauce
⅓ cup (80 ml) tomato sauce
olive oil, for shallow-frying
100 g thinly sliced Cheddar, cut into 24 squares, each 3 cm
24 baby rocket leaves, stems removed and torn into 2.5 cm pieces
12 cornichons (baby gherkins), cut into thin slices

1 Stamp out rounds from the burger buns using a 4 cm cutter; you should get 24 from the tops and 24 from the bases. If your buns are quite thick, trim them with a serrated knife after you have cut them.
2 Combine the beef mince, breadcrumbs, French shallots, mustard, Worcestershire sauce, 1 tablespoon of the tomato sauce and some salt and cracked black pepper in a bowl. Divide the mixture into 24 walnut-sized pieces. With wet hands, shape the pieces into balls, then flatten into patties.
3 Heat a large heavy-based frying pan with enough oil to just cover the bottom of the pan and cook the patties over medium heat for about 1 minute on each side, or until browned, then place on a baking tray.
4 Lightly grill both halves of the mini burger buns. Top each patty with a small slice of cheese and grill for 1 minute, or until the cheese is just starting to melt.
5 Place the patties on the bottom halves of the burger buns. Top with the rocket leaves, cornichon slices and the remaining tomato sauce. Gently press on the top half of the burger bun and secure with a cocktail stick through the middle. Serve warm.

NOTE: If you know an obliging baker, you can ask them to make 4 cm burger buns for you. Another alternative to using burger buns is to use Turkish bread.

THINK AHEAD: The uncooked hamburger patties can be frozen in single layers in an airtight container for up to 2 months. Thaw them before cooking.

Take a walnut-sized portion of the mince mixture and form it into a patty.

Put a small square of cheese on each patty and melt under the grill.

GRILLED FIGS IN PROSCIUTTO

Preparation time: 10 minutes
Cooking time: 15 minutes
Makes 24

50 g unsalted butter
2 tablespoons orange juice
6 small–medium fresh figs
6 long thin slices of prosciutto,
    trimmed of excess fat
24 sage leaves

1 Place the butter in a small heavy-based saucepan. Melt over low heat, then cook the butter for 8–10 minutes, or until the froth subsides and the milk solids appear as brown specks on the bottom of the saucepan. Strain the butter into a clean bowl by pouring it through a strainer lined with a clean tea towel or paper towel. Stir the orange juice into the strained butter.
2 Gently slice the figs lengthways into quarters. Cut each slice of prosciutto into four even strips. Sit a sage leaf on each fig segment, then wrap a piece of prosciutto around the middle of each one, with the ends tucked under the bottom of the fig. Arrange the figs, cut-side-up, on a baking tray and brush lightly with the butter mixture.
3 Move the grill tray to its lowest position, then preheat the grill to hot. Place the baking tray of figs on the grill tray and grill the figs for 1–1½ minutes, or until the prosciutto becomes slightly crispy. Serve hot or at room temperature. If you are serving the figs hot, provide serviettes to avoid burnt fingers.

NOTE: Because figs are a seasonal fruit, you will need to check their availability with your greengrocer before planning your menu. It is wise to buy a few extra figs than you think you will need because their delicate flesh is easily damaged in transport.
THINK AHEAD: The figs can be wrapped up to 6 hours in advance and covered in plastic wrap. Cook them just before serving.
VARIATION: You can adapt this recipe to make the popular party food snack, Devils on horseback by using pitted prunes instead of figs. Soak 24 wooden skewers in water for 30 minutes. Wrap a strip of prosciutto around each prune and secure with a skewer. Brush with the butter mixture and cook under a preheated grill for about 1 minute, or until the prosciutto goes crispy.
   Another favourite is Angels on horseback. It is very similar to Devils on horseback, but uses oysters instead of prunes. Either use 24 oysters on the shell or bottled oysters. Remove the oysters from their shells, or drain from the bottling liquid.

Strain the butter through a strainer lined with a clean tea towel.

Sit a sage leaf on a fig piece, then wrap a piece of prosciutto around the outside.

variations on a theme MINI PIES

No matter what the occasion, these pies will be a hit. Make your favourite filling and while it is cooling, prepare the pastry shells. Each filling makes enough for 24 mini pies.

BASIC PASTRY SHELL
750 g ready-made shortcrust pastry
1 egg, lightly beaten

Preheat the oven to moderate 180°C (350°F/Gas 4) and put a baking tray in the oven. Grease 24 mini muffin holes. Roll the pastry thinly and cut out 24 rounds with a 7 cm cutter. Repeat with a 5.5 cm cutter. Put one of the larger rounds in each muffin hole and fill with your cooled filling. Dampen the edges of the small rounds and place them on top of the filling to seal the pies. Brush with egg. Put the tin on the hot baking tray and cook for 25 minutes, or until golden. Cool slightly, then remove from the tin. Enough for 24 pies.

HINT: If you are serving a variety of the pies, decorate each pie with a different pastry shape on top so that you can identify them.

MOROCCAN LAMB
Ready in under 1 hour 45 minutes

2 tablespoons olive oil
1 onion, thinly sliced
2 cloves garlic, crushed
2 teaspoons ground cumin
2 teaspoons ground ginger
2 teaspoons paprika
1 teaspoon ground turmeric
1 teaspoon ground cinnamon
500 g lamb fillet, diced
1½ cups (375 ml) beef stock
1 tablespoon finely chopped
   preserved lemon
2 tablespoons sliced Kalamata olives
1 tablespoon chopped fresh coriander
24 pastry shells
plain yoghurt, to serve

Heat the oil in a large saucepan over medium heat, then add the onion, garlic and spices. Coat the lamb in the spice mixture, then pour in the stock, cover and cook over low heat for 30 minutes. Add the lemon and cook, uncovered, for a further 20 minutes, or until the liquid has reduced and the lamb is tender. Stir in the olives and coriander and allow to cool before filling the pastry shells. Cook for 25 minutes, then serve with the yoghurt.

RATATOUILLE
Ready in under 1 hour 15 minutes

¼ cup (60 ml) olive oil
1 eggplant, diced
1 onion, finely chopped
1 red capsicum, diced
1 small zucchini, diced
1 tablespoon tomato paste
200 g tomatoes, chopped
1 teaspoon dried Italian herbs
24 pastry shells
ready-made or home-made pesto
   from page 55, to serve

Heat 2 tablespoons of the oil in a frying pan and cook the eggplant until golden. Remove from the pan. Heat the remaining oil in the pan, add the onion, capsicum and zucchini and cook for 2 minutes. Stir in the tomato paste, fresh tomato, herbs and eggplant. Cook for 20 minutes, or until reduced. Cool, fill the pies, then cook for 25 minutes. Serve with pesto.

THAI CHICKEN CURRY
Ready in under 1 hour 15 minutes

1 tablespoon olive oil
1 small onion, finely chopped
2 cloves garlic, chopped
1 tablespoon finely chopped lemon grass, white part only
1½ tablespoons Thai curry paste
300 g diced skinned chicken breast
2 kaffir lime leaves
1½ cups (375 ml) coconut cream
1 tablespoon fish sauce
2 tablespoons finely chopped fresh coriander
24 pastry shells
sweet chilli sauce, to serve

Heat the olive oil in a large frying pan over medium heat, add the onion, garlic and lemon grass and cook, stirring, for 5 minutes. Stir in the curry paste, chicken, lime leaves and coconut cream and simmer for 20 minutes, or until the mixture has thickened. Remove the lime leaves with tongs, then stir in the fish sauce and fresh coriander. Cool the mixture, then fill the pies. Cook for 25 minutes, then serve with the chilli sauce.

BURGUNDY BEEF
Ready in under 2 hours 15 minutes

2 tablespoons olive oil
500 g diced lean beef (topside)
1 onion, finely chopped
50 g pancetta, finely chopped
2 cloves garlic, crushed
1 tablespoon tomato paste
1 cup (250 ml) red wine
½ cup (125 ml) beef stock
1 teaspoon dried Italian herbs
½ cup (125 g) puréed tomatoes
24 pastry shells

Heat half the oil in a large saucepan and cook the beef in batches over high heat for 5 minutes, or until browned. Remove the meat and set aside. Add the remaining oil and cook the onion, pancetta and garlic for 3–4 minutes, or until soft. Return the meat to the pan, stir in the rest of the ingredients, cover and simmer for 50–60 minutes, or until the meat is tender. Remove the lid and cook for a further 30 minutes, or until the sauce is reduced. Cool, fill the pies, then cook for 25 minutes.

THINK AHEAD: The fillings can be frozen for 1 month, then thawed. Or, you can cook the pies up to 2 days early and reheat in a warm (160°C/ 315°F/Gas 2–3) oven for 10 minutes.

From left: Moroccan lamb, Ratatouille, Thai chicken curry, Burgundy beef.

FETA CHOUX PUFFS

Preparation time: 30 minutes +
   cooling
Cooking time: 40 minutes
Makes 40

1 teaspoon cumin seeds
1/3 cup (80 ml) olive oil
3 cloves garlic, crushed
1 cup (125 g) flour, sifted
5 eggs
200 g feta, crumbled
1/2 quantity home-made (page 8) or
   140 g ready-made taramasalata
1/2 quantity home-made (page 9) or
   140 g ready-made baba ganouj

1 Preheat the oven to moderately hot 200°C (400°F/Gas 6). Toast the cumin seeds in a dry frying pan over low heat for 1–2 minutes, or until fragrant. Cool slightly then finely grind to a powder.

2 Heat the oil in a saucepan, add the garlic and ground cumin and cook over medium heat for 1 minute. Add 1 cup (250 ml) water and bring to the boil, then immediately remove from the heat and add the sifted flour all at once. Beat with a wooden spoon until smooth. Return to the heat and continue to beat for 2 minutes, or until the mixture forms a ball and leaves the side of the pan. Remove from the heat and transfer to a bowl. Cool for 5 minutes. Add the eggs, a little at a time, beating well between each addition, until thick and glossy—a wooden spoon should stand upright in it. If it is too runny, the egg has been added too quickly.

Beat for several minutes more, or until thickened. Stir in the feta.

3 Drop balls of the batter (about 1/2 tablespoon of batter) onto a lined baking tray. Bake for 10 minutes, then reduce the heat to moderate 180°C (350°F/Gas 4) and cook for a further 20 minutes. Turn the oven off and remove the puffs. Using the tip of a small paring knife, cut a small slice halfway through the puffs. Return

to the oven and leave for 10 minutes with the oven door slightly ajar.

4 When the puffs have cooled and dried out, fill half with taramasalata and the rest with baba ganouj. To do this, spoon the taramasalata into a piping bag fitted with a small plain nozzle or fill the corner of a plastic bag, cut a hole in the corner and squeeze into the puffs. Repeat with the baba ganouj.

Stir the batter constantly until it comes away from the side of the pan.

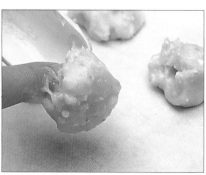

Drop small dollops of the batter on a lined baking tray.

Pipe the filling into the puffs, using baba ganouj for half and taramasalata for half.

MEXICAN BITES

Preparation time: 40 minutes +
  30 minutes refrigeration
Cooking time: 5 minutes
Makes 36

740 g can kidney beans, drained
1 teaspoon ground cumin
2 tablespoons olive oil
¼ teaspoon cayenne pepper
1 avocado
1 small clove garlic, crushed
2 tablespoons sour cream
2 tablespoons lime juice
1 vine-ripened tomato, seeded
  and finely chopped

2 tablespoons finely chopped fresh
  coriander
250 g packet round tortilla chips

1 To make the refried beans, put the kidney beans in a bowl and mash well with a potato masher, then add the cumin. Heat 1½ tablespoons of oil in a large non-stick frying pan and add the cayenne pepper and mashed kidney beans. Cook over medium–high heat for 2–3 minutes, stirring constantly. Allow to cool, then refrigerate for about 30 minutes, or until cold.
2 Scoop the avocado flesh into a food processor and add the garlic, sour cream and 1 tablespoon of the

lime juice. Process for a few minutes until it is a thick creamy paste, then add salt to taste. Refrigerate.
3 To make the salsa, mix together the tomato, coriander and the remaining oil and lime juice in a bowl. Refrigerate until needed.
4 To assemble, lay out 36 round tortilla chips. Put a heaped teaspoon of refried beans in the centre of each chip, add a teaspoon of the avocado cream and lastly half a teaspoon of tomato salsa.

THINK AHEAD: The bean purée can be made 3 days in advance. Make the salsa up to 2 hours beforehand. Assemble just before serving.

Mash the red kidney beans with a potato masher.

Blend the avocado mixture until a thick, creamy paste is formed.

Make the salsa by combining the tomato, coriander, oil and lemon juice.

PRAWN, NOODLE AND NORI PARCELS

Preparation time: 45 minutes
Cooking time: 20 minutes
Makes 24

Dipping sauce
1/3 cup (80 ml) tonkatsu sauce or
   barbecue sauce (see Note)
2 tablespoons lemon juice
1 tablespoon sake or mirin (see Note)
1–2 teaspoons grated fresh ginger

250 g dried somen noodles
3 sheets nori (dried seaweed)
1/2 cup (60 g) plain flour
2 egg yolks
24 raw medium prawns, peeled and
   deveined with the tails intact
oil, for deep-frying

1 Mix the dipping sauce ingredients in a small bowl, adding the ginger according to taste.
2 Using a sharp knife, cut the noodles to the same length as the prawn bodies (from the head to the base of the tail). Keep the noodles in neat bundles and set aside. Cut the nori into 2.5 cm wide strips.
3 Sift the flour into a large bowl and make a well in the centre. Mix the egg yolks with 1/4 cup (60 ml) of water. Gradually add to the flour, whisking to make a smooth lump-free batter. Add another tablespoon of water if the mixture is too thick.
4 Dip a prawn in the batter, letting the excess run off. Roll the prawn lengthways in noodles to coat it with a single layer. Keep the noodles in place by rolling a nori strip around the centre of the prawn and securing it with a little batter. Repeat with the rest of the prawns.
5 Fill a deep heavy-based saucepan or deep-fryer one third full of oil and heat to 180°C (350°F), or until a cube of bread browns in 15 seconds. Deep-fry 2–3 prawns at a time, for about 1–2 minutes, or until the prawns are cooked. Drain on crumpled paper towels and keep warm while cooking the remainder. Serve warm with the dipping sauce.

NOTE: Nori, tonkatsu sauce, sake and mirin are all Japanese ingredients. You can find them at Asian speciality stores.
THINK AHEAD: You can make the sauce in advance, but the prawns are best done close to serving time.

Cut the noodles into strips approximately the same length as the prawn bodies.

Roll the prawns in noodle strips so that the body is covered.

Roll a strip of nori around the middle to secure the noodles.

WILD MUSHROOM PATE ON MELBA TOASTS

Preparation time: 30 minutes +
2 hours soaking + 3 hours
refrigeration
Cooking time: 15 minutes
Makes 30

20 g dried wild mixed forest
mushrooms (e.g. cep, chanterelles,
black chanterelles)
50 g butter
375 g flat mushrooms, sliced
1 garlic clove, crushed
2 tablespoons brandy
1/4 cup (60 ml) thick cream
1 teaspoon fresh thyme
1/4 teaspoon juniper berries, ground
100 g ready-made mini Melba toasts
crème fraîche, to serve
30 fresh flat-leaf parsley leaves

1 Soak the dried mushrooms in a
bowl with 1 cup (250 ml) hot (not
boiling) water for 2 hours, or until
soft. Drain, reserving 2 tablespoons
of the soaking liquid. Discard any
pieces of mushroom that are still
tough and woody after soaking.
2 Melt the butter in a large frying
pan over medium heat, then add
the flat mushrooms and sauté for
5 minutes. Add the garlic and cook
for 1 minute, then add the dried
mushrooms and reserved soaking
liquid and cook for another
5–8 minutes, stirring regularly.
Pour in the brandy and cook for
2 minutes, or until evaporated.
Remove from the heat and allow to
cool for 10 minutes.
3 Transfer the cooled mushroom
mixture to a food processor with the
cream, thyme, ground juniper berries
and 1/2 teaspoon each of salt and
cracked black pepper and blend for
4–5 minutes, or until finely chopped.
4 Spoon the pâté into a bowl and
refrigerate, covered, for at least
3 hours, or until chilled. Dollop a
teaspoon of pâté on each toast and
top each toast with 1/2 teaspoon
crème fraîche and a fresh parsley leaf.

THINK AHEAD: The pâté can be
made up to 3 days early and stored
in the fridge in an airtight container.
Spread the pâté on the toasts just
before serving.

*Stir the mushrooms regularly while they
are being cooked.*

*Blend the mushroom mixture in a food
processor until finely chopped.*

PEKING DUCK ROLLS

Preparation time: 35 minutes +
   10 minutes resting
Cooking time: 5 minutes
Makes 24

1 cup (125 g) plain flour
½ teaspoon sesame oil
½ large Chinese roast duck
6 spring onions, cut into 6 cm lengths
   (24 pieces in total)
1 Lebanese cucumber, seeded and
   cut into 6 cm x 5 mm batons
2–3 tablespoons hoisin sauce
2 teaspoons toasted sesame seeds
24 chives, blanched

1 Sift the flour into a small bowl, make a well in the centre, and pour in the sesame oil and ½ cup (125 ml) boiling water. Mix well until the mixture becomes a slightly sticky soft dough. If needed, add a few teaspoons more of boiling water at a time if the mixture is still a bit dry. Knead the dough on a floured work surface for about 5 minutes, or until smooth. Cover and rest for about 10 minutes.

2 Shred the duck meat into pieces with your fingers and cut the skin into small strips.

3 Roll the dough into a sausage shape and divide into 24 pieces, then roll each piece to an 8–9 cm round with a rolling pin on a lightly floured board. Once they are rolled out, lay them out in a single layer and cover with plastic wrap or a tea towel while you are rolling out the others to prevent them from drying out.

4 To cook the pancakes, heat a non-stick frying pan over medium–high heat, and dry fry them in batches for about 20 seconds each side. Do not overcook, or they will become too crispy for rolling. The pancakes should have slight brown speckles on them. Stack each pancake on a plate, and keep warm. If they cool down too much, reheat by wrapping them in foil and baking in a warm (170°C/325°F/Gas 3) oven until warmed through, or microwave for

20–30 seconds on high.

5 Arrange a piece of spring onion, cucumber, duck flesh and skin on each pancake. Drizzle with ½ teaspoon hoisin sauce and sprinkle with sesame seeds. Roll up firmly and tie each pancake with a blanched chive strip.

THINK AHEAD: You can make the pancakes 2–3 days ahead of time; wrap them tightly in plastic wrap until ready to serve. Reheat them by wrapping them in foil and baking in a warm (170°C/325°F/Gas 3) oven until warmed through, or microwave for 20–30 seconds on high.

Roll each portion of dough into a neat round with a rolling pin.

Tightly roll the pancakes to enclose the filling, then secure with a blanched chive.

GYOZA

Preparation time: 30 minutes
Cooking time: 30 minutes
Makes 45

300 g pork mince
250 g finely shredded and lightly
    blanched Chinese cabbage with
    the excess water squeezed out
60 g fresh Chinese chives, chopped
1 tablespoon finely chopped fresh
    ginger
¼ cup (60 ml) soy sauce
1 tablespoon rice wine
1 teaspoon sugar
45 gow gee wrappers
2 teaspoons oil

Dipping sauce
2 tablespoons soy sauce
1 tablespoon black Chinese vinegar
1 teaspoon sesame oil
½ teaspoon chilli oil

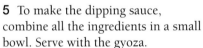

1 Place the pork mince, Chinese cabbage, Chinese chives and ginger in a bowl and mix together. Add the soy sauce, rice wine, sugar and 1 teaspoon salt to the mixture and mix together very well.
2 Place a gow gee wrapper flat in the palm of your hand, then, using your other hand, place 2 teaspoons of the filling mixture into the centre of the wrapper. With wet fingers, bring the sides together to form a half-moon shape and pinch the seam firmly to seal it in a pleat.
3 Press one side of the dumplings onto a flat surface to create a flat bottom; this will make the dumplings

easier to pan-fry.
4 Heat the oil in a frying pan over medium–high heat. Add the gyoza to the pan in batches and cook for 1–2 minutes on the flat side, without moving, so that the gyoza become brown and crisp on that side. Transfer to a plate. Return the gyoza to the pan in batches, then gradually add 100 ml water to the pan and put the lid on. Steam for 5 minutes. Empty the pan and wipe it dry between batches.

5 To make the dipping sauce, combine all the ingredients in a small bowl. Serve with the gyoza.

THINK AHEAD: You can make the filling a day before assembling the dumplings. Alternatively, the filling can be made and frozen for up to 3 months. Thaw it completely before assembling the dumplings.

Place 2 teaspoons of the filling into the middle of the gow gee wrapper.

Pinch the seam of the gyoza firmly to seal it in a pleat.

Cook the gyoza, flat-side-down, in batches without turning.

GRILLED PRAWNS WITH TEQUILA MAYONNAISE

Preparation time: 20 minutes +
    1 hour marinating
Cooking time: 15 minutes
Makes 24

24 raw king prawns
1/3 cup (80 ml) olive oil
2 tablespoons lime juice
1 tablespoon tequila
2/3 cup (160 g) whole-egg
    mayonnaise

1 Peel and devein the prawns, keeping the tails intact. Combine the olive oil with the lime juice and season with salt and cracked black pepper. Add the prawns and leave to marinate for 1 hour.
2 Meanwhile, mix the tequila into the mayonnaise, then transfer to a serving dish.
3 Heat a barbecue or chargrill pan to hot, add the prawns and cook for 1–2 minutes on each side until pink and cooked through. Serve with the tequila mayonnaise for dipping.

THINK AHEAD: The prawns can be grilled up to an hour beforehand. One way to save time is to buy pre-cooked prawns from your fishmonger. Then all you need to do is to peel them, leaving the tails intact. Squeeze them with lime juice and serve with the mayonnaise.

VARIATION: If you prefer to have a dipping sauce without alcohol, simply add 2 tablespoons of chopped fresh herbs, such as dill, basil or parsley to the mayonnaise instead of the tequila.

Alternatively, add a teaspoon of grated lemon or lime rind for a fresh citrus flavour.

Remove the vein from the prawns, starting at the head end.

Add the tequila to the mayonnaise and mix together well.

SAVOURY SHORTBREAD WITH TOMATO JAM

Preparation time: 30 minutes +
2 hours refrigeration
Cooking time: 3 hours
Makes 48

Tomato jam
5 vine-ripened tomatoes, quartered
1 teaspoon fennel seeds
½ teaspoon cumin seeds
1 small red onion
2 cloves garlic
100 ml olive oil
1½ tablespoons soft brown sugar
1½ tablespoons red wine vinegar

Shortbread
250 g butter, at room temperature
1 tablespoon hot water
3¼ cups (405 g) plain flour
½ teaspoon sweet paprika
300 g bacon, finely chopped
1¼ cups (125 g) grated Parmesan
60 g poppy seeds
small fresh basil leaves, to garnish

1 Preheat the oven to moderate 180°C (350°F/Gas 4). Place the tomatoes on a roasting tray and roast for 30 minutes. Cool slightly, then purée in a blender or food processor until just smooth. Toast the fennel and cumin seeds in a dry frying pan for 1–2 minutes, or until fragrant. Cool slightly, then grind the seeds to a powder.
2 Purée the onion, garlic, ground spices and half the olive oil in a food processor until well combined.
3 Heat the remaining olive oil in a large saucepan and cook the onion mixture over low heat for 25–30 minutes, or until the onion is just beginning to caramelise. Add the sugar and vinegar and cook for a further 2 minutes, then stir in the tomato mixture. Cook over very low heat, stirring occasionally, for 1–1½ hours, or until the paste is thick and there is very little liquid remaining. Remove from the heat and allow to cool.
4 To make the shortbread, beat the

butter in a bowl until pale. Gradually add the hot water. Sift the flour and paprika into the bowl and mix with a wooden spoon until smooth. Stir in the bacon, Parmesan and ¼ cup (60 ml) water, then season well with cracked black pepper, adding more water if necessary. Roll into four logs 3 cm thick. Wrap in plastic wrap and refrigerate for 2 hours. Spread the poppy seeds out on a clean work surface and roll the logs in them until evenly coated.
5 Preheat the oven to warm 170°C (325°F/Gas 3) and lightly grease two baking trays. Slice the logs into 5 mm

thick slices. Place on the prepared trays and bake for 15–18 minutes, or until pale and crisp. Cool completely.
6 To serve the shortbread, top with 1 teaspoon tomato jam and a small basil leaf.

THINK AHEAD: The jam will keep for up to 4 weeks in the refrigerator. The shortbread can be made up to 1 week in advance and stored in single layers in an airtight container.
VARIATIONS: Grated Cheddar, chopped fresh herbs, finely chopped nuts or a spice mix can be used to flavour the dough.

Cook the tomato jam until it is thick and most of the liquid has evaporated.

Roll each of the shortbread logs in the poppy seeds.

variations on a theme BRUSCHETTA

A great way to fill up your guests is to make plenty of bruschetta—it's easy and universally popular. And once you get the hang of it, you can use almost any topping.

BASIC BREAD BASE

1 loaf Italian bread
1 large clove garlic, peeled
extra virgin olive oil, to drizzle

Preheat the oven to moderately hot 200°C (400°F/Gas 6). Slice the loaf of bread on the diagonal into twelve 1 cm thick slices. Lay the bread slices out in a single layer on a baking tray and bake for 10–12 minutes, or until they are lightly golden. Remove from the oven and rub the garlic clove over one side of each slice of toast. Lightly drizzle each slice with extra virgin olive oil, then cut them in half again so that each piece is easily handled by your guests. Add your choice of topping and serve.

NOTE: Bruschetta are best made at the last moment to prevent the bread drying out or the toppings from making the bread soggy.

SALMON TARTARE WITH FRIED CAPERS
Ready in under 30 minutes

1 tablespoon olive oil
2 tablespoons baby capers
300 g sashimi salmon, finely diced
1½ tablespoons whole-egg mayonnaise
3 teaspoons lime juice
2 teaspoons chopped fresh dill
24 bruschetta slices
1 lime, skin and pith removed and individual segments separated

Heat the oil in a frying pan and cook the capers for 1–2 minutes, or until crisp. Remove with a slotted spoon and drain on crumpled paper towels. Place the salmon in a bowl with the mayonnaise, lime juice and dill, then season with salt and pepper. Spoon the tartare onto the bruschetta and top with capers and a lime segment.

SMOKED TURKEY, PEAR AND WALNUTS
Ready in under 30 minutes

¼ cup (60 g) whole-egg mayonnaise
1 clove garlic, crushed
1 tablespoon sherry
2 teaspoons wholegrain mustard
2 teaspoons chopped fresh oregano
200 g thinly sliced smoked turkey, roughly chopped
1 ripe pear, cored and cut into thin wedges
2/3 cup (85 g) chopped roasted walnuts
24 bruschetta slices
24 fresh oregano leaves

Place the mayonnaise, garlic, sherry, mustard and oregano in a small bowl and mix well. Put the turkey in another bowl with the pear and walnuts. Stir the mayonnaise mixture through the pear and walnut mixture

until well combined, then season with salt and pepper. Spoon onto the prepared bruschetta and top with an oregano leaf. Serve immediately.

FETA, ROCKET AND MUSHROOM
Ready in under 30 minutes

1 tablespoon olive oil
60 g butter
300 g small Swiss brown mushrooms, cut into quarters
2 cloves garlic, crushed
1/4 cup (7 g) roughly torn fresh basil
150 g soft marinated feta
50 g baby rocket leaves
24 bruschetta slices

Heat the oil and butter in a frying pan over high heat until the butter has melted, then add the mushrooms and cook for 3–4 minutes. Add the garlic and cook for a further minute. Remove the pan from the heat and stir in the basil, then season with some salt and cracked black pepper. Spread the feta on the prepared

bruschetta, then add a few rocket leaves. To finish, top with some of the fried mushrooms, and serve immediately.

TOMATO AND BASIL
Ready in under 30 minutes

3 large (400 g) vine-ripened tomatoes, cut into 1 cm pieces
1/4 cup (60 ml) extra virgin olive oil
1/3 cup (10 g) fresh basil, torn into small pieces
24 bruschetta slices

Place the tomato slices in a bowl with the extra virgin olive oil and torn basil. Season with plenty of salt and cracked black pepper and toss together until well combined. Spoon the mixture onto the prepared bruschetta slices and serve immediately.

VARIATION: A simple alternative to these toppings is to lightly sprinkle the prepared bruschetta with some fresh or dried chopped herbs.

From left: Salmon tartare with fried capers, Smoked turkey, pear and walnuts, Feta, rocket and mushroom, Tomato and basil.

MINI SPICY PORK QUESADILLAS

Preparation time: 45 minutes
Cooking time: 40 minutes
Makes 24

2¾ tablespoons olive oil
½ teaspoon ground oregano
1 teaspoon ground cumin
½ teaspoon garlic salt
½ teaspoon cayenne pepper
350 g pork mince
2–3 chopped jalapeño chillies
    in brine
¼ cup (30 g) pitted black olives,
    sliced
⅓ cup (55 g) green olives stuffed with
    red pimentos, sliced
2 tablespoons chopped fresh
    coriander leaves
12 x 16 cm flour tortillas
½ cup (60 g) grated mild Cheddar
½ cup (75 g) grated mozzarella
fresh coriander sprigs, to garnish

1 To make the spicy pork mince, heat 1½ tablespoons of the olive oil in a large frying pan; when hot add the oregano, cumin, garlic salt and cayenne pepper and cook for 30 seconds. Add the pork mince and cook over high heat for 10 minutes, before incorporating the chillies and all the olives. Cook for another 5 minutes, then stir in the chopped coriander. Remove from the heat and allow to cool.

2 Cut each tortilla in half. Place 1 tablespoon of filling on one half of each half. Mix the cheeses together, then put 1 tablespoon of the grated cheese on top of the spicy pork mince. Turn the flap of tortilla over the filling and press down firmly.

3 Heat 2 teaspoons of the remaining oil in a non-stick frying pan over high heat and cook the quesadillas in batches of six for 3–4 minutes each side, or until golden. Add a teaspoon of oil to the pan after each batch. Garnish with coriander sprigs.

THINK AHEAD: The spicy pork mince can be made in advance and refrigerated for up to 3 days.
VARIATION: For a very simple vegetarian filling, simply sprinkle each half tortilla with 1 tablespoon chopped tomato, chilli, olives and coriander, then the cheese; fold over and cook as for the pork quesadillas.

Stir the chopped coriander into the spicy pork mixture.

Fold the flap of the tortilla so that it covers the filling.

BLOODY MARY OYSTER SHOTS

Preparation time: 10 minutes +
 30 minutes refrigeration
Cooking time: Nil
Serves 12

⅓ cup (80 ml) vodka
½ cup (125 ml) tomato juice
1 tablespoon lemon juice
dash of Worcestershire sauce
2 drops of Tabasco
pinch of celery salt
12 oysters
1 cucumber, peeled, seeded and
 finely julienned

1 Combine the vodka, tomato juice, lemon juice, Worcestershire sauce, Tabasco and celery salt in a jug. Mix well, then refrigerate for 30 minutes, or until chilled. Just before serving,

fill each shot glass about two thirds full. Drop an oyster in each glass, then top with a teaspoon of julienned cucumber. For the final touch, crack some black pepper over the top of each shot glass, then serve.

NOTE: It is better to use oysters fresh from the shell rather than from a jar because they have a much better, fresher taste.

Finely shred the peeled and seeded cucumber with a sharp knife.

THINK AHEAD: The tomato mixture can be made a day ahead of time and kept in the fridge. Stir before serving.
VARIATION: If you think your guests are game enough for some fire in their evening, make chilled sake shots—fill each glass two thirds full of sake, add an oyster, then garnish with cucumber.

Fill each glass about two thirds full, then drop in an oyster.

HERBED PIKELETS WITH PEAR AND BLUE CHEESE TOPPING

Preparation time: 20 minutes
Cooking time: 15 minutes
Makes 36

1 cup (125 g) self-raising flour
2 eggs, lightly beaten
½ cup (125 ml) milk
2 tablespoons finely chopped
    fresh parsley
2 teaspoons finely chopped fresh sage

Pear and blue cheese topping
100 g Blue Castello or other creamy
    blue cheese
75 g cream cheese
2 teaspoons brandy
1 large ripe green-skinned pear
¼ cup (30 g) toasted walnuts, finely
    chopped
½ lemon
30 g chives, cut into 3–4 cm lengths

1 To make the pikelets, sift the flour into a bowl and make a well in the centre. Gradually add the combined eggs and milk, mixing the flour in slowly. When the flour is incorporated, add the parsley and sage and season well with salt and cracked black pepper. Whisk well until a smooth batter forms.

2 Heat a large non-stick frying pan over medium heat and spray the surface with cooking oil spray. Drop heaped teaspoons of batter into the pan and flatten them a little to give 5 cm circles. Cook until bubbles appear in the surface of the pikelet,

then turn and brown the other side. Lift out to cool on a wire rack.

3 To make the topping, beat the cheeses and brandy together until smooth. Season with pepper. Cut the pear in half and peel and core one half of it, then dice it into 5 mm pieces, leaving the rest of the pear untouched. Stir the diced pear into the cheese mixture along with the walnuts. Core the other half of the pear but do not peel it. Slice the pear into thin slices along its length (so that each slice has one border with the skin on). Cut these into 2 cm

triangles with one slightly curved side having green skin. Squeeze some lemon juice over the cut surfaces to prevent discoloration.

4 Pile 1 teaspoon of topping in the centre of each pikelet and flatten it slightly to cover most of the surface. Arrange three of the pear triangles on top in a row, overlapping one another. Garnish with chives.

THINK AHEAD: The pikelets can be made 1 day in advance. Store in an airtight container in the fridge. Assemble 1 hour before serving.

Cook the pikelets until bubbles form on the surface, then turn over.

Stir the walnuts and diced pear through the soft cheese mixture.

Cut the pear into neat triangles, each with one strip of the green skin.

CHOC-DIPPED ICE CREAM BALLS

Preparation time: 30 minutes + freezing
Cooking time: 10 minutes
Makes 36

500 g good-quality ice cream (use vanilla or a mixture of vanilla, pistachio and chocolate)
150 g dark chocolate
150 g white chocolate
150 g milk chocolate
2 tablespoons toasted shelled walnuts, roughly chopped
2 tablespoons shelled pistachios, roughly chopped
2 tablespoons toasted shredded coconut

1 Line two large baking trays with baking paper and place in the freezer to chill. Working quickly, use a melon baller to form 36 balls of ice cream and place on the chilled baking trays. Place a cocktail stick in each ice cream ball. Return to the freezer for 1 hour to freeze hard.
2 Place the chocolate in three separate heatproof bowls. Bring a saucepan of water to the boil, then remove the pan from the heat. Sit one bowl at a time over the pan, making sure the base of the bowl does not sit in the water. Stir occasionally until the chocolate has melted. Remove the bowl from the heat and set aside to cool; the chocolate should remain liquid; if it hardens, repeat.
3 Put the walnuts, pistachios and coconut in three separate small bowls. Working with 12 of the ice cream balls, dip one at a time quickly in the dark chocolate, then into the bowl with the walnuts. Return to the freezer. Repeat the process with another 12 balls, dipping them in the melted white chocolate and the pistachios. Dip the last 12 balls in the milk chocolate, then the toasted coconut. Freeze all the ice cream balls for 1 hour.

THINK AHEAD: Ice cream balls can be prepared up to 2 weeks in advance and kept in a single layer in an airtight container.

Scoop ice cream balls with a melon baller and place on chilled baking trays.

Dip the ice cream balls in the melted dark chocolate.

Dip the chocolate-covered balls in the toasted walnuts.

HAZELNUT BISCOTTI WITH FRANGELICO SHOTS

Preparation time: 20 minutes +
    20 minutes cooling
Cooking time: 45 minutes
Makes 40

1 3/4 cups (215 g) plain flour
2/3 cup (160 g) caster sugar
1/2 teaspoon baking powder
60 g chilled unsalted butter, cubed
2 eggs
1 1/4 cups (150 g) roughly chopped
    roasted hazelnuts
2 teaspoons grated orange rind
1/2 teaspoon caster sugar, extra

Frangelico shot
1/4 cup (60 ml) double-strength coffee
    per person
1–2 teaspoons Frangelico per person

1 Preheat the oven to moderate 180°C (350°F/Gas 4) and line two baking trays with baking paper. Place the sifted flour, sugar, baking powder and a pinch of salt in a food processor and mix for 1–2 seconds. Add the butter and mix until the mixture resembles fine breadcrumbs. Add the eggs and process until the mixture comes together.
2 Transfer the dough to a floured surface and knead in the hazelnuts and orange rind. Divide into two equal portions and, using lightly floured hands, shape each into a log about 20 cm long. Place the logs on the baking trays and sprinkle with the extra sugar. Press the top of each log down gently to flatten slightly.

3 Bake for about 20 minutes, or until golden. Remove and set aside to cool for about 20 minutes. Reduce the oven temperature to warm 160°C (315°F/Gas 2–3).
4 Cut the logs into 5 mm–1 cm slices on the diagonal (at least 6 cm long). Turn the baking paper over, then spread the biscotti on the tray in a single layer. Return to the oven and bake for a further 20–25 minutes, or until they just begin to colour. Cool

completely before storing in an airtight container.
5 To make the Frangelico shot, pour hot coffee into shot glasses and top with Frangelico to taste.

THINK AHEAD: Store the biscotti in an airtight container for 1 month.
VARIATION: Use whole toasted almonds instead of the hazelnuts and replace the Frangelico with Amaretto in the coffee shots.

Mix the batter in a food processor until it starts to resemble fine breadcrumbs.

Shape the dough into two long logs, each about the same size.

Use a serrated knife to slice the logs slightly on the diagonal.

MINI CHERRY GALETTES

Preparation time: 30 minutes
Cooking time: 30 minutes
Makes 30

670 g jar pitted morello cherries, drained
30 g unsalted butter
1½ tablespoons caster sugar
1 egg yolk
½ teaspoon vanilla essence
½ cup (95 g) ground almonds
1 tablespoon plain flour
2 sheets ready-rolled puff pastry, thawed
icing sugar, for dusting
½ cup (160 g) cherry jam

1 Preheat the oven to moderate 180°C (350°F/Gas 4). Line a baking tray with baking paper. Spread the cherries onto several sheets of paper towel to absorb any excess liquid. Combine the butter and sugar in a bowl and beat until creamy. Add the egg yolk and vanilla, then stir in the combined almonds and flour and refrigerate until required.

2 Cut 30 rounds from the pastry sheets using a 5 cm round cutter. Place half the rounds on the prepared tray and lightly prick them all over with a fork. Cover with another sheet of baking paper and weigh down with another baking tray—this prevents the pastry from rising during cooking. Cook for 10 minutes,

remove from the oven and allow to cool on the trays. Repeat with the remaining rounds. Leave the oven on.

3 Place 1 level teaspoon of almond mixture in the centre of each cooled pastry round, then press three cherries onto the almond mixture.

4 Bake for another 10 minutes or until lightly browned. Cool slightly then dust lightly with icing sugar. Place the jam in a cup, stand in a saucepan of hot water and stir until melted. Glaze the cherries by brushing them with the warmed jam.

THINK AHEAD: The almond topping can be prepared up to 4 days in advance. Assemble on the day of the party so that they don't go soggy.

Beat the butter and sugar together until a creamy consistency is reached.

Prick each of the pastry rounds with the tines of a fork.

Firmly press three cherries onto the almond mixture.

101

MINI MUD CAKES

Preparation time: 1 hour
Cooking time: 35 minutes
Makes 30

3/4 cup (185 g) caster sugar
175 g dark chocolate, chopped
90 g unsalted butter, chopped
2 eggs, lightly beaten
2 tablespoons brandy
1/2 cup (60 g) plain flour
1/2 cup (60 g) self-raising flour
1/4 cup (30 g) cocoa powder
50 g milk chocolate melts
200 g dark chocolate melts, chopped
1/2 cup (125 ml) cream

1 Preheat the oven to moderate 180°C (350°F/Gas 4). Lightly grease the base and sides of a 20 cm x 30 cm baking tin. Cover the base and two long sides with baking paper. Place the sugar, chocolate, butter and 1/4 cup (60 ml) water in a small saucepan and stir over low heat for about 5 minutes, or until the chocolate has melted. Remove from the heat, cool to room temperature then stir in the eggs and brandy.
2 Sift the flours and cocoa into a bowl and make a well in the centre. Pour the chocolate mixture into the well. Mix and pour into the prepared tin. Bake for about 20–25 minutes, or until a skewer inserted into the centre comes out clean. Cool in the tin for 5 minutes before inverting onto a wire cake rack to cool.
3 Dip a 3 cm round cutter in hot water and cut out 30 rounds of cake, re-dipping the cutter between each round (this makes a neater edge). Roll the cut surface gently on the bench to press in any crumbs. Place the little cakes, top-side-down, on a wire cake rack over an oven tray.
4 To make chocolate curls, place the milk chocolate melts in a heatproof bowl. Bring a saucepan of water to the boil, then remove the pan from the heat. Sit the bowl over the pan, making sure the base of the bowl does not sit in the water. Stir occasionally until the chocolate has

melted. Spread the chocolate fairly thinly over a marble board or cool baking tray and leave at room temperature until just set. Using the edge of a sharp knife at a 45 degree angle, scrape over the top of the chocolate. The strips will curl as they come away—don't press too hard. If the chocolate has set too firmly, the curls will break. Leave in a warm place and try again.
5 Place the dark chocolate melts in a bowl. Heat the cream until almost boiling and pour over the chocolate;

leave for 2 minutes, then stir until the chocolate melts and is smooth. Spoon the chocolate mixture evenly over the cakes, reheating gently if it becomes too thick. Tap the tray gently to settle the chocolate, top each cake with a chocolate curl and allow to set. Use a palette knife to remove from the cake rack.

THINK AHEAD: Un-iced mud cakes will keep in an airtight container for 3 days in a cool place or for 2 months in the freezer.

Roll the cake rounds on the bench so that the crumbs are pushed in.

Scrape the chocolate with a sharp knife at a 45 degree angle.

LEMON CURD AND BLUEBERRY TARTLETS

Preparation time: 20 minutes
Total cooking time: 45 minutes
Makes 48

150 ml lemon juice
2 teaspoons finely grated lemon rind
6 egg yolks
1/2 cup (125 g) sugar
100 g butter, diced
4 sheets ready-made shortcrust pastry (24 cm x 24 cm)
2 tablespoons icing sugar
48 blueberries

1 Whisk together the lemon juice, rind, egg yolks and sugar, then cook in a saucepan over low heat for 2–3 minutes, or until the sugar has dissolved. Gradually add the butter, stirring continuously, and cook for 8–10 minutes, or until thick. Remove from the heat and cover the surface with plastic wrap to prevent a skin forming. Refrigerate until needed.
2 Preheat the oven to moderate 180°C (350°F/Gas 4) and lightly grease 24 x 3 cm tartlet tins. Cut 48 rounds from the pastry with a 5 cm cutter and line the tins with half of them. Lay the other rounds on a lined baking tray, cover with plastic wrap and refrigerate until needed. Bake the cases for 12–15 minutes, or until golden. Allow to cool completely. Repeat with the remaining rounds.
3 When cool, dust each tartlet with icing sugar and spoon 1 teaspoon curd into each one; top with a blueberry.

THINK AHEAD: The cases can be baked up to 1 week in advance and stored in an airtight container. To revive them, heat in a moderate (180°C/350°F/Gas 4) oven for 5 minutes. The curd can be made 2 days ahead. Assemble no more than 1 hour before serving.

Whisk the lemon juice, lemon rind, egg yolks and sugar together.

Cook the lemon curd mixture until it thickens.

Line the tartlet tins with the small rounds of pastry.

GRAPE FRITTERS WITH CINNAMON SUGAR

Preparation time: 10 minutes
Cooking time: 20 minutes
Makes 24

Cinnamon sugar
2 tablespoons caster sugar
1 teaspoon ground cinnamon

2 eggs, separated
1/2 teaspoon vanilla essence
1/4 cup (60 g) caster sugar
150 g seedless red or black grapes
1/3 cup (40 g) self-raising flour
40 g unsalted butter

1 To make the cinnamon sugar, combine the sugar and cinnamon in a bowl.

2 Whisk the egg yolks with the vanilla and sugar until combined and just creamy. Slice each grape into four slices, then stir the grape slices into the egg yolk mixture. Sift the flour into the egg mixture. Beat the egg whites in a clean bowl until soft peaks form. Lightly fold half of the egg whites into the egg yolk mixture with a metal spoon until just combined, then repeat with the rest of the egg whites.

3 Melt 2 teaspoons of the butter in a frying pan over low heat. Place 6 separate heaped teaspoons of the batter into the pan to make six fritters. Cook over low–medium heat for 2–3 minutes, turning very carefully when the base becomes firm and bubbles appear around the edges. Flip gently and cook for a further 1–2 minutes, or until golden. Remove to a plate and keep warm. Repeat three more times to make 24 fritters. Dust the warm fritters with cinnamon sugar and serve warm.

THINK AHEAD: The fritters are best made as close to serving as possible on the day they are to be served. If necessary, they can be heated in a warm (170°C/325°F/Gas 3) oven for 5 minutes. Sprinkle them with sugar just before serving.

Cut all of the grapes into four slices with a sharp knife.

Gently fold the egg whites through the rest of the fritter mixture.

MINI ECLAIRS

Preparation time: 30 minutes
Cooking time: 30 minutes
Makes 24

60 g unsalted butter, chopped
1 cup (125 g) plain flour, sifted
4 eggs, beaten
300 ml cream
1 tablespoon icing sugar, sifted
½ teaspoon vanilla essence
50 g dark chocolate

1 Preheat the oven to moderately hot 200°C (400°F/Gas 6) and line two baking trays with baking paper. Put the butter in a small saucepan with 1 cup (250 ml) water. Stir over low heat until melted. Bring to the boil, then immediately remove from the heat and add the flour all at once. Beat with a wooden spoon until smooth. Return to the heat and beat for 2 minutes, or until the mixture forms a ball and leaves the side of the pan. Remove from the heat and transfer to a bowl. Cool for 5 minutes. Add the egg, a little at a time, beating well between each addition, until thick and glossy—a wooden spoon should stand upright.

2 Spoon the mixture into a piping bag with a 1.2 cm plain nozzle (you might need to do it in batches). Pipe 6 cm lengths of batter on the baking trays. Bake for 10 minutes, then reduce the heat to moderate 180°C (350°F/Gas 4) and cook for another 10 minutes, or until golden and puffed. Split the eclairs and remove the soft dough from the middle with your fingers or a small spoon. Return to the oven for 2–3 minutes to dry out a little more. Cool on a wire rack.

3 Pour the cream into a bowl and add the icing sugar and vanilla. Whip until thick. Spoon into a piping bag and pipe into the bottom of each eclair. Replace the eclair pastry tops.

4 Place the chocolate in a heatproof bowl. Bring a saucepan of water to the boil, then remove the pan from the heat. Sit the bowl over the pan; make sure the base does not sit in the water. Stir occasionally until melted.

5 Spoon the chocolate into a small plastic bag and push into a corner. Snip a small hole in the corner and drizzle stripes over each eclair. Serve.

Stir the flour mixture over the heat until it comes away from the side of the pan.

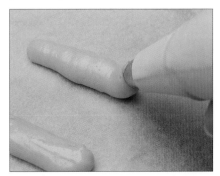

Pipe strips of the eclair batter on two lined baking trays.

Pipe the whipped cream into the bottom half of the eclairs.

APRICOT AND COCONUT MACAROONS

Preparation time: 20 minutes
Cooking time: 30 minutes
Makes about 45

3 egg whites
1¾ cups (435 g) caster sugar
1¼ cups (115 g) desiccated coconut
½ cup (125 g) finely chopped glacé apricots
1½ tablespoons plain flour
icing sugar, for dusting

1 Preheat the oven to slow 150°C (300°F/Gas 2). Line a baking tray with baking paper. Combine the egg whites and sugar in a bowl and place over a saucepan of simmering water over low heat, making sure the base of the bowl does not touch the water. Whisk for about 5 minutes, or until thick and glossy. Do not overheat or the whites will cook. Allow to cool slightly, then fold in the coconut, apricots and flour. Mix well. The mixture should be firm enough to pipe.
2 Spoon the warm mixture into a large piping bag fitted with a 1 cm plain tube. Pipe 3 cm round mounds on the baking tray, leaving about 3 cm between each mound. With a wet finger, gently press the top down, so it doesn't overbrown during baking.
3 Bake for about 18–20 minutes or until light brown all over, then cool on the trays. Dust the tops lightly with icing sugar before serving.

NOTE: If you don't have a piping bag, use a plastic bag and snip 1 cm

off one of the corners; you will probably need to do it in two batches.
THINK AHEAD: The macaroons will keep for up to 3 days if they are stored in an airtight container.

VARIATION: Dip the bases of the cold macaroons in 150 g melted dark chocolate, wipe the excess off on the side of the bowl, and place the macaroons on baking paper to set.

Whisk the egg whites and sugar until thick and glossy.

Fold the coconut, apricots and flour into the egg white mixture.

Pipe 3 cm rounds of the mixture onto a lined baking tray.

FENNEL WAFERS

Preparation time: 45 minutes +
  30 minutes refrigeration
Cooking time: 10 minutes
Makes about 40

¼ cup (60 g) sugar
2 tablespoons sesame seeds
2 tablespoons fennel seeds
1½ cups (185 g) plain flour
¼ cup (60 ml) olive oil
¼ cup (60 ml) beer
1 tablespoon anisette liqueur

1 Preheat the oven to moderately hot 200°C (400°F/Gas 6). Lightly grease a baking tray and line with baking paper. In a small bowl, combine the sugar, sesame seeds and fennel seeds.
2 Sift the flour and a pinch of salt into a large bowl and make a well in the centre. Add the oil, beer and liqueur and mix with a large metal spoon until the dough comes together.
3 Transfer the dough to a lightly floured surface and knead until elastic. Wrap the dough in plastic wrap and refrigerate for 30 minutes. Divide the dough in two and roll each portion out between two sheets of baking paper as thinly as possible. Stamp rounds out of the dough using a 4 cm round cutter; you should get about 40 rounds.
4 Sprinkle the dough rounds with the sugar mixture, then gently roll a rolling pin over the top of them so that the seeds adhere to the dough.
5 Transfer the rounds to a baking tray and cook for 6–8 minutes. Put the wafers under a hot grill for 1–2 minutes to caramelise the sugar, taking care not to burn them. Transfer to a wire rack and allow to cool.

THINK AHEAD: The wafers will keep in an airtight container for up to 2 weeks.

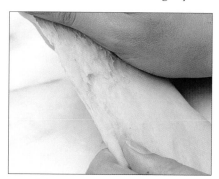

Knead the dough until it is smooth and elastic.

Stamp out rounds of the dough with a 5 cm cutter.

Sprinkle the sugar mixture over the uncooked wafers.

MENU IDEAS

If you're dazzled by the possibilities, here is a selection to help you get started. Use the lists as a basis for the menu at your next party.

CHAMPAGNE BREAKFAST/BRUNCH

Fresh juices and seasonal fruits will provide the setting for a perfect brunch. Round out the menu with mini croissants, muffins or brioche.

MENU 1

16 Buckwheat blini with smoked salmon

28 Rolled omelette with ocean trout caviar

54 Quail eggs with spiced salts ∨

65 Asparagus and prosciutto bundles with hollandaise

67 Petit croque-monsieur

104 Grape fritters with cinnamon sugar ∨

MENU 2

20 Mini bisteeya

32 Creamed egg tartlets with roe

52 Rösti with smoked trout and salsa verde

97 Bloody Mary oyster shots

98 Herbed pikelets with pear and blue cheese topping ∨

103 Lemon curd and blueberry tartlets ∨

OUTDOOR SUMMER DRINKS

A selection of food perfect for a midsummer drinks party. Keep it cool and light and don't overload on the alcohol on a hot day.

MENU 1

18 Chicken san choy bau

21 Cucumber cups with Thai beef salad

26 Salt and pepper squid

40 Oysters with ginger shallot dressing

45 Vietnamese rice paper rolls

56 Thai fish cakes with dipping sauce

MENU 2

8 Guacamole with (**14**) Tortilla shards ∨

36 Salt cod fritters

41 Oysters with tomato, chilli and coriander salsa

87 Mexican bites ∨

92 Grilled prawns with tequila mayonnaise

96 Mini spicy pork quesadillas

ELEGANT EVENING CELEBRATION

No mess allowed for the most special of occasions. Grown-up food for discerning palates. Set the tone with succulent oysters.

MENU 1

40 Oysters with lemon herb dressing

28 Rolled omelette with ocean trout caviar

47 Scallops on potato crisps with pea purée

72 Dressed-up baby potatoes ∨

83 Grilled figs in prosciutto

100 Hazelnut biscotti with Frangelico shots ∨

MENU 2

33 Asian-flavoured crab tartlets

41 Oysters with wasabi crème fraîche

54 Quail eggs with spiced salts ∨

75 Layered sushi

90 Peking duck rolls

103 Lemon curd and blueberry tartlets ∨

AFTERNOON TEA

Not necessarily what your grandmother would have made, but there are some classics in this selection of nibbles. Serve on delicate china plates.

PORTABLE CANAPÉS

Finger food that can be prepared completely in advance and transported easily. Take platters, bowls and napkins and arrange the food when you find the perfect spot.

QUICK AND EASY

For food that gets you out of the kitchen as soon as possible, choose these menus and round them out with some ready-made treats from the delicatessen.

MENU 1

16 Buckwheat blini with smoked salmon

31 Rare roast beef on croûtes

55 Roast vegetable and goat's cheese roulade V

67 Smoked trout tea sandwiches

105 Mini eclairs V

106 Apricot and coconut macaroons V

MENU 2

25 Capsicum muffins with tapenade and mascarpone V

49 Turkish bread with herbed zucchini V

61 Goat's cheese, walnut and beetroot crepe rolls V

78 Mini roasted vegetable frittatas V

101 Mini cherry galettes V

102 Mini mud cakes V

MENU 1

10 White bean dip with (**15**) Herb grissini V

17 Stuffed black olives V

37 Dolmades V

78 Mini roasted vegetable frittatas V

84 Moroccan lamb pies

107 Fennel wafers V

MENU 2

35 Thai chicken sausage rolls

45 Vietnamese rice paper rolls

48 Honey mustard chicken drumettes

54 Quail eggs with spiced salts V

74–75 Sushi

106 Apricot and coconut macaroons V

MENU 1

8 Guacamole V

24 Spicy corn puffs V

44 Macadamia-crusted chicken strips with mango salsa

77 Sesame and wasabi-crusted tuna cubes

92 Grilled prawns with tequila mayonnaise

97 Bloody Mary oyster shots

MENU 2

10 White bean dip V

40 Oysters with lemon herb dressing

48 Honey mustard chicken drumettes

71 Zucchini and haloumi fritters V

83 Grilled figs in prosciutto

95 Tomato and basil bruschetta V

V *indicates vegetarian food or food with a vegetarian option.*

INDEX

This edition published in 2009 by Bay Books, an imprint of Murdoch Books Pty Limited.
Pier 8/9, Hickson Road, Millers Point, NSW 2000, Australia.

Managing Editor: Rachel Carter
Editor: Zoë Harpham
Creative Director: Marylouise Brammer
Designers: Annette Fitzgerald, Norman Baptista
Food Director: Jane Lawson
Food Editor: Christine Osmond
Recipe Development: Alison Adams, Jane Charlton, Rebecca Clancy,
Ross Dobson, Michelle Earl, Jo Glynn, Jane Griffiths, Katy Holder, Kathy Knudsen,
Jane Lawson, Valli Little, Christine Osmond, Wendy Quisumbing, Jo Richardson
Home Economists: Alison Adams, Renée Aiken, Rekha Arnott,
Justin Finlay, Valli Little, Kim Passenger, Angela Tregonning
Photographers: Cris Cordeiro, Rob Reichenfeld, Ian Hofstetter (cover), Oliver Ford (steps)
Food Stylists: Carolyn Fienberg, Mary Harris (cover)
Food Preparation: Briget Palmer, Alison Adams (steps), Kim Passenger (steps),
Margot Smithyman (steps), Angela Tregonning (steps)

Chief Executive: Juliet Rogers.
Publisher: Kay Scarlett.

ISBN 978 0 681 02053 5
Printed by Sing Cheong Printing Co. Ltd. PRINTED IN CHINA.

INTERNATIONAL GLOSSARY OF INGREDIENTS

capsicum	red or green pepper	fresh coriander	fresh cilantro
eggplant	aubergine	tomato purée (Aus.)	sieved crushed tomatoes/
tomato paste (Aus.)	tomato purée, double		passata (UK)
	concentrate (UK)	zucchini	courgette